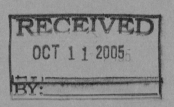
MAIN

startling
joy

startling joy

Seven Magical Stories
of Christmas

James Calvin Schaap

Revell

Grand Rapids, Michigan

Published by Fleming H. Revell
a division of Baker Publishing Group
P.O. Box 6287, Grand Rapids, MI 49516-6287

Printed in the United States of America

Library of Congress Cataloging-in-Publication Data
Schaap, James C., 1948-
    Startling joy : seven magical stories of Christmas / James Calvin Schaap.
        p.   cm.
    ISBN 0-8007-1877-1 (cloth)
    1. Christmas stories, American. 2. Christian fiction, American. I. Title.
PS3569.C33S73 2005
813′.54—dc22   2005008430

You've Been Searching for Joy . . .

Who hasn't? It's Christmas. So where's the goodwill? Where's the love? Would you recognize them if you saw them? Maybe you ought to **Prepare for the Unexpected** (page 7). Or unravel Christmas joy as in **The Mystery** (page 11). Someone says you can get a glimpse in the face of **The Baby** (page 19) at the local nativity. But you're not sure you'll make it. There's **The Party** (page 31). And there are presents to buy. Finding just the right ones takes time, sometimes a lifetime, says that mom who knows all about **The Gifts** (page 57). Maybe if you look at **The Church** (page 85). Surely there's joy there. Remember that time you saw it in the faces of the children at **The Pageant** (page 99). How wonderful that is, like **The Afterglow** (page 113) when all those you love and enjoy most have been round you. What if you could find that joy all over again? What if joy like that would descend, covering you and everyone you know like **The Snowfall** (page 141)—what then? What then? **Wouldn't it change everything?**

Prepare for the Unexpected

A Foreword

Most of the stories in this book end at beginnings. The last story ends with the last prayer of the Bible, one of the best beginnings an ending ever had: "Come, Lord Jesus."

What better beginning than the coming of the Christ? Into our lives, into the world, his second coming ever fulfilling his first?

The character who prays that final prayer has just begun to know a personal, spiritual poverty which knowledge is the perfect preparation for Jesus.

Another character, a young girl standing outside the church at the end of her story, for the first time recognizes the baby Jesus in her arms, recognizes the Christ in the greater story of Christmas.

Another character, a grown woman, by watching the moment a new mother first meets her adopted baby, is persuaded to remember her own motherhood, and so begins grandmotherhood in hope and love.

And a grandmother's story ends just as her granddaughter says, for the first time ever, to the swelling of the old woman's heart: "I want to see Jesus."

There is a pattern here.

Jim Schaap writes about those common relationships that all of us have experienced. He knows our lives, re-fires our memories. He draws us into settings familiar. He causes us to inhabit the worlds of plain folk struggling with the problems of an ordinary life—and he makes it all so very, very important, for this is the place where humanity happens. We love and fail and work and hurt and grow here. And as all these stories revolve around Christmas and the incarnation, here too is where God comes to meet us, at which we make our best beginnings.

That is part of the pattern too. More than making them merely "important," Schaap writes sacred mystery into our common lives. Every one of his stories brings us, his willing readers, to a holy *anagnorisis*.

This Greek word generally means "recognition." Aristotle used it to describe that moment in a tragedy when some startling discovery by a character produces a change from ignorance to knowledge—and knowledge reverses the character's life thereafter. In tragedy, that reversal is for the worst. Near the end of his play, Oedipus the king discovers to his horror that the woman he married is in fact the woman who bore him long ago. He has married his mother.

In Schaap's stories the *anagnorisis*, the "recognition," is ever and altogether the opposite. Lives leap toward their beginnings. Characters caught in struggles that bid fair to bury them (our grandmother, just minutes before her granddaughter wanted to "see Jesus," had wished "that she were with Jack [her deceased husband] and the Lord"); characters in various forms of troubled ignorance; characters grown helpless all suddenly discover, by means most ordinary and familiar, that "Jesus . . . he's always there."

Perhaps a better word than *anagnorisis* is *epiphany*. James Joyce used it to describe certain recognitions in his stories; but his epiphanies often disabused a character of some illusion. They showed reality to be a hard, impenetrable, unforthcoming thing.

Jim Schaap, however, uses this word in his very last story as it has been used by the Christian Church from its beginning: to describe the startling discovery that Christ can shine in the common things. The Lord of glory flashes forth! And reality grows sacred, the handiwork of God, the stuff that contained the Word, the Son of God.

I'll quote Schaap: "And that's when it hit me, this epiphany of Christmas. He came for those who need him, not because they are poor or slovenly or unable to care for themselves. He came for . . . some like me, self-satisfied with . . . arrogance. He came for me because I too—in my annoyance and my pride—am very much among the needy."

And then: "The Lord of heaven and earth was acting upon me. Come, Lord Jesus."

So ends the book, with the beginnings of a startling, everlasting joy.

Walter Wangerin Jr.
March 2005

The Mystery

A Preface

It's so cold outside that the bus windows are sealed in frost, and I don't see this monstrosity of a bus driver until the very second the doors swish open and she yelps at me to watch my step on the way up.

"My daughter's laid up right now in pain something fierce with a strained ligament," she says, "and I wouldn't bless something like that on my worst enemy."

She's so huge that her bulk hangs from the edge of the driver's seat the way a blanket of melting snow leans over a roof on a sunny day. Her legs have been poured into a pair of fancy black Levis; the seams have been nailed shut, fortunately, by a line of brass rivets that run up from her boots to her waist. Her shirt is embroidered with squiggles and sequins down her forearms, her cuffs have mother-of-pearl snaps, and she's left her wide collar slanting open halfway to her navel, as if someone should care.

The bus is nearly full. I take a seat up front, one of the only ones left. I've been in her presence for all of ten seconds, but I've no trouble knowing why that's the only seat left: everyone else has taken cover.

"She was only stepping off a curb is all," the driver says, "and something went ping in her leg. Just like that, she went down."

I'm thinking that this is a university shuttle bus I've just boarded, and one is not supposed to find these types on university buses, where meditative silence reigns. Her jabber is an affront, an embarrassment, especially since it's aimed right at me. Her voice ricochets into the far reaches of the vehicle, and I pull out the latest campus paper, open it wide to cover my eyes.

"'Course, I know about those things too," she says. "I lived through a torn ligament myself once—bring you a mess of pain, all right. People say a good sprain is sometimes worse than a break. You know what I'm saying?"

Like it or not, she's zeroed in on me, jawing away as if I'd been her neighbor since the war—any of them. She's pushing sixty, I'm guessing—if you can read between the thick lines of eye shadow and the heavy splash of rouge that turns her puffy face into a Halloween mask. Her hair is nothing more or less than flat orange, and she's wearing this broad-brimmed cowboy hat with a flush of feathers jutting out from the right side of her head like the wing of a dead chicken.

"That was a whole lot of pain, that was. Kept me off my feet for far too long, I'll tell you."

I get the feeling that I'm going to be told, whether or not it's in my own best interest.

"That was back in my younger days. I didn't always keep such good records back then, and here if one night two guys don't show up for me at the same time." Her shoulders heave when she laughs and remembers. She stamps on the gas, and we lurch out from the curb. "So anyway, I'm upstairs with Alvin, see, and here if I don't hear the front doorbell. So I lean out the window, and what'll you know if it's not another guy downstairs come for me." She looks at

13

me in the mirror and raises one fat finger up to her lips as if mum's still the word on all this.

"I'm somewhere between a rock and a hard place," she says with a few more spicy words between. "So I got to try to make ends meet somehow, see? So I climb out on the roof to get away from Alvin. I sure didn't want him to know who was down there and why, but I got to get to the door for Bernie. Well, so as to make a long story short, I came up lame—turned an ankle when I come shimmying down the gutter."

I'm thinking of my children's talking clown. You give the cord a long jerk, and the doll jabbers until the cord gets gobbled up into its back. This one's got no cord that I can see.

"The odd thing is I end up that night with Bernie, the guy downstairs, if you can believe it. Of course, Alvin is my ex-husband." She says it proudly, face up, as if she's trying to catch some midsummer sunshine through the windshield of the bus.

It dawns on me then that I've stumbled on Chaucer's Wife of Bath.

She reaches back and flips her hair out of the back of her collar. "Can't help but feel sorry for my daughter this time, though—what with the tough time she's had, just leaving her husband like she did."

14

It makes no difference whether we're stopped at a light or cruising along through rush-hour traffic, the monologue roars on.

"I told her she never should've married that guy. Long as they was living together, everything was hunky-dory. But once she married him, that was it. He starts beating on her, see." She raises a fist as broad as a new cement block. "I don't know why anybody'd want to get married. Before my daughter got hitched to that guy, he never laid a hand on her," she says. "That slip of paper is all they need to think they own you."

I looked up at her mirror at the very second she gunned her eyes up at me, so I shrugged my shoulders when she looked for my reaction. I wasn't up to a fight with her.

"You think I'm lying?" she says. "Marriage is an institution, all right."

Now I see that her story is meant as a parable for the two cow-eyed students snuggling up to each other across the aisle. I could take her on, of course—give her a lecture on compassionate and nurturing marriage—but I've got only six blocks to go. "Whatever you say," I tell her.

"Now, you take my boyfriend," she says. "I love that man, all right, but I don't think I'll marry him. I'd sure as anything move in with him, but I won't marry him. No, sirreee."

Somewhere in this city, I'm thinking, there's a man who's fearfully and wonderfully blessed.

"Trouble is, he won't move in with me, see?" she says. "He's a sweetheart of a guy, and I just love him to death, I'll tell you."

I can't lose now, I figure. We're a block from my stop. "He won't move in with you?" I ask the mirror.

"Nope," she says, shaking her head as if it's just unheard of.

The gravel cracks when we get to the place where I'll step off the bus. She hits the brakes as if she wants every single passenger front and center on a dime.

"Why won't he?" I say, shouldering a bag full of books as I get to my feet. The young-and-in-love stand too, equally interested.

She tips back her hat and squints right up at me standing there at the front of the bus. "He's too stinking religious," she says, cranking the door open for us to leave. "Have a nice day now, you hear?"

Once my car's heater throws out warm air, I start to think about this December cowgirl and her too-

16

religious sweetheart. And here's what I come up with: the strange thing about her story is nothing more or less than the miracle of the incarnation. Even the over-weight, obnoxious, promiscuous, over-the-hill cowgirl bus driver somehow plays host to the parasite power of the Word-made-flesh, who is working in her too, even today, through a boyfriend with saintly scruples. It's as if Christ wants her, even if no one else on the bus does, and even if she's not so hot on him.

The miracle of the incarnation is that Christ himself pulled on a suit of human flesh and laid himself down in a barn, all for the likes of us—the cowgirl bus driver, in all her ribald excesses, and her arrogant passenger, the distinguished professor with all his button-down sophistication. For the publican and the Pharisee.

He's come to us, for us. He's come—amazingly, shockingly—because he loves us.

That's the startling joy of Christmas.

1 . . . The Baby

Forgetting Jesus

Just one of the bad things about eighth grade, Gina thought, was having to stand up in front of church in the Sunday school Christmas program like a giant right in the middle of the munchkins.

People really came to see the little kids, she thought. On Christmas Eve the church was packed with grandpas and grandmas sitting there like a bunch of geese craning their necks to see what their little sweeties were doing on stage—pulling a face or waving or taking a bite out of the hems of their skirts.

And where did Nelvie Richter come from every year, anyway? Nobody would see her all year long, it seemed, and then suddenly at Christmas she'd appear like some kind of angel, she and her bullhorn, to take charge of the program. She'd never married, was probably forty already, and had run the Christmas program ever since the Bible was written, at least.

But this year Nelvie had chosen Gina to be Mary, which wasn't really a bad deal, Gina figured, since for the most part it meant sitting down near the manger instead of being an angel and having to stand there like a skyscraper.

Being Mary meant not having to recite any Bible verses or anything like that either. All you had to do, Nelvie said, was sit there on the floor and look at the baby while Donny Lemkull, a sixth grader with glasses, read Luke 2 for the one-hundred-and-sixty-seventh time. Donny claimed he wanted to be a medical missionary someday, and everybody believed him.

On three Sunday mornings they practiced instead of having Sunday school. Nelvie would stand up behind the communion table and yell out commands through that bullhorn. "Third graders, pay attention!" "Gregg Annenburg, turn around!" "Sixth graders, what's so terribly funny?" Gina would sit on the stage with her legs beneath her, figuring there must be thirty thousand kids in Sunday school, all of them buzzing around like bugs. It was enough to make her never want to be a mom.

"Whose baby you going to have up here?" Gregg asked that first Sunday.

Nelvie told him that it would be a doll, of course, not a real baby.

On Christmas Eve, fifteen minutes before the program, most of the eighth graders sat on the soft chairs in the youth room, trying to stay out of the way of the stars, the little kids, who were all duded up but flying around anyway as if shot out of guns. Everywhere you looked, teachers were running around trying to round them up, like a church rodeo.

"So what does it feel like to be a mom?" Gregg said. He was a shepherd himself, holding this long stick he must have picked up in the woods somewhere.

The truth was she hadn't thought about being Mary at all. "What do you care?" she said.

"Well, excuse me for living," he said, rolling his eyes.

And that's when Nelvie came in. She had on a red dress, cut kind of low, Gina thought. "I don't have a Jesus," she said. "I forgot him completely." She said it as if she were making this big confession and she didn't care who heard. "We've got to have a Jesus."

That's when she pointed. "Gina," she said, "you live closest. Can you run home and find a doll?"

"It better be a boy," Gregg said.

Gina rummaged through her mind to try to find one. It couldn't be a Barbie, of course. But it had been years since she'd played with a real doll, one of those little ones with eyes that flop closed when you laid them in your arms.

"I'll get my mom," she said.

"You don't have time," Nelvie said. "Just run. It would take you too long to get them out of church and everything."

When Gina stood up her hands went down almost instinctively to her robe. "Like this?"

"Sure," Nelvie said, "it's okay."

Outside the snow fell in fleecy clumps, floated down as if somewhere not so far up above the clouds were tipped with feathers. She raised her skirt with her right hand, clutched the shawl around her neck in her left, and watched the light snow puff up from her footfalls as she ran down two blocks of sidewalks all the way home. A doll, she thought—some kind of doll.

She unlocked the door, using the extra key above the light, ran quickly upstairs, and fumbled through the

24

closet in her bedroom. Teddy bears, stuffed animals, Garfield—there was plenty of kid's stuff around but no plain baby. She couldn't remember having one, really, one of those little ones, one with a hole in her lips where she takes a bottle. She'd never had one, she thought. She wished she'd told Nelvie right then and there. She wished she had dared to tell her somehow that this was a wild goose chase. Barbies she had galore, but she didn't remember a real baby.

The whole program was waiting for her now, everybody sitting there in church wondering. She felt almost like crying, though she didn't know why. She looked down at her watch. It was still ten-to—she didn't have to panic.

A baby. One of those little dolls, the soft ones. She'd had one once, along with a carriage, a little buggy with wire wheels falling apart. Sure, that canopy-like thing was all torn, she remembered, worn out from years in the sun or something. It was her mother's buggy and her mother's doll—it had a plastic face and plastic hair and little dabs of red in its nostrils. And when you lifted up the skirt there was nothing underneath but cloth. It had plastic legs and plastic arms and a plastic head, but its body was just something sewn, like a pillow.

25

She slapped the lights off in her bedroom and ran back down the hall toward the closet at the top of the stairs. If it was around at all, it would have to be there—with her father's crutches from the time he broke his leg and her mother's old cheerleading megaphone, and the box of pictures and army clothes and all of that.

She pulled the chair away from the closet door and reached inside for the light. When she pulled the string, immediately she saw the buggy behind the dusty old aquarium. She wriggled herself into the closet and wormed her way toward the back, stepping over her brother's trombone and a hatbox full of old checks in rubber bands. She reached into the buggy, her shawl still up around her shoulders, and felt the baby.

With the light behind her, she could barely see the doll, but she knew it was naked. It had to have a blanket, of course, something for a baby. She pulled it into her shawl and held it beside her as she backed out of the closet, trying to guess where she might find something to wrap it in.

What came to her mind were the old diapers her mother used as rags. They'd be in the kitchen closet ragbag, lots of them. Every time somebody spilled at supper, one of the old diapers, ripped and torn and worn half to shreds, would be used for a mop. She ran downstairs, the baby in one arm, her skirt in the other hand, flicking out lights with her elbow.

When she reached in the bag she pulled out a handful, torn and crumpled but perfectly clean and fluffy. She spread them out on the table and laid the doll inside, then wrapped it up firmly, four or five old diapers wound around it as if it might somehow be cold. It would have been better to have a real blanket, she thought, something new and pretty. But the old diapers would have to do this time. Five minutes, the kitchen clock said.

She punched in the door lock before she shut the front door and wound the baby into her shawl, arranging the diapers so that its face was open to her own. She couldn't run in that long skirt because it took both arms to hold the baby. So she walked, telling herself that the show could go on without her, that the manger scene wouldn't come until most of the little kids were already swept off the stage.

She walked quietly in the brightness of the snow against the darkness of the night, the tiny bundle in her arms seeming as if it were something of her own, not her mother's—something real. It felt strange to hold, wrapped like it was in those swaddling clothes, and she laughed to think of it—the diapers like those real swaddling clothes in the story, the diapers around the baby from the closet. There was something like music in that idea, she thought, something making harmony in her mind and in her heart, something that made her smile and almost cry at the very same time, something so strange that she was almost ashamed to think it and yet so good that she wanted to tell all the world.

She had the baby, and the whole church was full of people, waiting. And they were all going to have to wait for her because this was the Prince, after all, and everyone always waits for the Prince. None of what they were doing in that church made any sense without this child, this little old doll in her arms, and she knew it. All of it was silly. If she would choose not to go now, she thought—if she just stayed outside here in the perfect peace of the night, in the soft shower of snow—she would make it all clear to them that without the child everything in that church was dumb. They'd all wonder why they'd come.

The whole church would sit through the parade of children, the proud grandparents picking out their own, and the little kids would blast out the chorus of "Christmas Bells," just like they'd done at practice, screaming only on the words they knew. Once that was over, the whole church would wait for the manger scene.

But it wouldn't come. They'd wait longer, some of them growing impatient finally and looking at each other, wondering why the whole night was not moving along the way it should. Then someone somewhere would get the message that there was no baby. People would begin to whisper to themselves, then talk out loud, turn around, and look at the back as if something terrible had occurred. Nelvie would stand with her hands over her face. Gregg would roll his eyes, embarrassed. Everything would stop. Everything. And all because Gina had the baby in her arms.

She looked down at the baby's face and swept the snow away from its forehead as she walked. Up ahead, the church shone brightly in its own bath of light, and as she came closer she heard the organ and the piano, just as she'd heard them practiced, a medley of carols ringing into the night through the slowly falling snow.

So she stood there looking up against the broad white sides of the church, and then she walked into the snow between the front sidewalks and stood there in her dark robe and shawl, holding the child in the bright lights that swept up from the ground and illuminated the sign on the lawn. She stood there as if she were the only one on the stage, the music filling in around her, making her feel something that she somehow understood to be her own very first Christmas Eve.

She recognized the baby Jesus in her mother's old doll from the closet, in the swaddling clothes she'd wrapped him in herself, and even in the way the Mary she'd become was just now pondering all of this in her heart. She felt it all, the child and the mother and the God who came from heaven to an old barn like a dusty closet. It all seemed so clear as she stood there on her own stage in front of church.

And that's where Nelvie Richter found her, just a few minutes later, in tears and smiling.

2 . . . The Party

Facts of Life

Countless times I've watched Verona Worth dole out extra chicken strips to Mandy, her granddaughter, the only third grader in Greenwood School she wouldn't dare to touch. I've worked with Verona ever since she started in the lunchroom, and a hundred times, I bet, I've seen her dawdle over a cup of applesauce just to keep Mandy at the window for an extra second. Sometimes she'll scrape beans off trays for twenty minutes on the chance the girl will give her only the slightest glance when she files by the tubs of dirty silverware.

Every noon Verona stands a countertop away from that child and sees her own son's eyes—strong and bright and quick, blue as heaven. And when she does, what she feels is written so deeply on the lines of her face that it doesn't take a gypsy to read it, only another grandma. She loves that child, even though Mandy doesn't know her from Martha Eshuis or Sylvia Brantsen or any of the girls who work the lunch lines with us.

Mandy is my granddaughter too, my seventh, out of twelve in all. She's the daughter of my daughter Kelly—and Verona's son Jeff, who wouldn't marry Kelly, even though my daughter surely would have had him. But in the lunchroom the whole business has never come up between us, even though Verona and I work side by side, baking chicken, spooning chocolate pudding into the Charlie Brown pies, and scrubbing out pots once the sixth grade is through the line at 12:30.

It happened at college, like so much does, and the night Jeff and Kelly told me and my husband, Verona came too, alone, like she's been since her husband died trucking, killed on an interstate in Utah, I think, or maybe Nevada. My daughter was pregnant, we found out, but Ted and I had jumped the gun ourselves way back in the olden days, so I'd been through some of that hurt myself, even though it's a whole lot worse when it's your daughter, let me tell you.

I love my Kelly and I always have, but she's been a chore to bring up, headstrong as she was from the moment she wouldn't take a binkie. But that night it wasn't Kelly who scared me, it was Verona, who sat with her legs crossed in a rocker beneath the clock and couldn't stop crying. She didn't bawl really, just whimpered constantly, kept dabbing at her eyes, so that whatever she said, or tried to say, came out off-key.

She'd taken Jeff over to our house to apologize to us because he'd already made it clear for reasons all his own that he wasn't about to marry my daughter. Lord knows Verona tried to do everything right, tried with a passion, but she was so broken that night, all she could do was mumble.

We never talk about little Mandy on the job, even though what happened is eight years behind us. It never comes up because Verona is embarrassed about what her son did to my Kelly. But that isn't all of it. She's embarrassed about that night too, about how she couldn't do much at all but slobber when she tried to be the mother—and the father—Jeff never had.

I feel the same way around the nurse who stood by me when my son Tom was born. When that boy didn't want to come, I made a horrible ruckus. If I see that nurse on the street—even today—I look away. She saw me in a state I'm not proud of, the way I saw Verona pinched in the rocking chair, in perfectly helpless pain over her only child.

Jeff's gone on to be someone, but he's never married, and if you ask me he doesn't pay much attention to his mother or his daughter. He lives in Virginia and works in Washington, D.C., does something with numbers—financial, works for the government, Verona says.

My Kelly took the next best thing once Jeff turned his back on her. When Mandy was a year old, Kelly married Reggie Ellenson, who stands first in line to inherit his father's masonry business. Reg never went to college. He's a fine man, but Kelly runs him, and she knew darn well she would. There's already two little boys—two little masons—behind Mandy, the princess she had with Jeff. I'm not proud of saying this, but I pray more for my Kelly today than I did eight years ago, the night she told us she was going to have a baby. My daughter is not finished growing up, even if she doesn't know it herself.

She came over Tuesday, mad as ever, because Verona had sent Mandy a new dress for her birthday. Verona's sent things anonymously for years—at Christmas she writes "Santa Claus" on the tag. First, it was rattles, then stuffed animals. The last few years it's been clothes, school clothes.

"You've got to do something about it, Mom," Kelly told me.

She stood at the door and didn't even unbutton her jacket, left the car running in the driveway, the boys inside. "It's driving me nuts, I swear it. Mandy's getting old enough so that I'm going to have to explain it, you know. Here this big package comes in the mail." She draws the lines with her arms. "The boys don't get anything extra. Mandy's going to wonder—you know she will."

"What can I do?" I said.

"You know her. You talk to her every day at school. Tell her she's got to stop—it's for Mandy's own good, Mom."

Like I said, I've seen Verona's long face whenever that darling Mandy walks by with an empty tray. Ever since the girl's been in kindergarten I've seen that look on Verona's face.

"I've talked to Reg's lawyers—the business, you know—and they claim I can get a court order—"

"My goodness, Kelly," I said.

"Listen to me! They said I can get a court order that would keep her from contacting Mandy in any way. It's the law."

"You going to arrest her for sending a pair of socks?"

"If I have to," she said.

Somewhere it's written, I think, that once the kids leave the nest a mother's supposed to stop worrying. You think that's the way it's going to be, but it isn't.

"You want me to tell her?" I said.

"I'm right about this, Mom. Maybe someday when Mandy's old enough, you know, when she can take the truth. But she's only eight years old." She ran her fingers through her hair like she always does, front to back, her father's thick dark hair. She's beautiful, my prettiest daughter. I've never quite figured out where she came from—such a beautiful girl at the end of the line.

"Mom," she says, "please? I just can't think of Christmas in another two weeks. Besides, she's getting so extravagant. This outfit must have cost sixty bucks."

"What was it?" I said.

She rolled her eyes. "What difference does it make?"

"Really?" I said. "Tell me about it."

She let out this long, grieved breath. "A black cotton jumper with suspenders and a bright yellow tube belt—"

"Sounds cute," I said.

"She even sent a pair of tights and a turtleneck."

I waited for her critique. "Well?" I said.

"I just won't have it anymore," she said. "I don't care if it's cashmere. You've got to tell her."

"Why me?" I said.

"It's either you or the lawyer."

Her father used to say that if Kelly got up a head of steam, she could carry the Chicago Bears on her back and still get where she wanted to go. In her entire life, the only thing she wanted but never got was Jeff Worth.

On Mondays we spread more peanut butter sandwiches than we normally do because sometimes kids don't get enough to eat over the weekend. Of everything we do in the kitchen, spreading sandwiches takes the most time. We go through more than a gallon of peanut butter every day.

Verona and I sat there together for almost an hour while the others were out setting tables and getting the lines ready. It was almost 11:00, time for the second grade to show up. The vegetables were already up in the roasters, ready to serve. It was almost Christmas now, but we were talking about the March menus. Planning school meals isn't any different from doing the job at home—it's hard to come up with something new. And it's got to be likeable, of course. The waste here is a sin you never quite get used to.

"We could use tons of apples," Verona said.

Sometimes government fruits come thick during the winter, if there's a surplus.

"You never know if we'll get them for sure," I told her.

"You never know anything for sure," Verona said.

"You got me there, I guess."

It was already the fourteenth. I knew that if I was ever going to say a thing, I had to do it now. I kept telling myself it was me or the lawyers. Kelly doesn't just shoot off her mouth about things like that. So I charged in right there in the middle of menus, and maybe I shouldn't have. Like I said, we've never said a word about Mandy before.

"Verona," I told her, "Kelly says that jumper you sent for Mandy's birthday was just darling."

You could feel cold seep into the room, as if someone had just opened a window to winter.

"I've been waiting to see it on her," I told her. "She looks so cute in dark colors."

Government peanut butter isn't the texture of Peter Pan. Sometimes toward the bottom of the can it spreads in chunks and rips the bread. She was being very careful.

"Verona," I said, "I wish there was some other way we could do this. I know what that child means to you. I mean, I can see it when she comes through the line."

She wasn't looking at me at all. She reached in the bag and pulled out a half dozen slices of bread, then jammed the spatula down into the tub for more peanut butter.

"I know we never talk about it," I said, "but if it helps at all for me to say it, I think I know how you feel."

41

"How dare you say that?" she said, turning to me, her eyes full of glass shards.

It was pointless for me to argue, so I let it go, and the both of us kept on spreading.

Martha finished up on the tables and came up to the window, wondering if she ought to start slicing up cheese for tomorrow's lasagna. When I told her to check the napkin holders, she knew something was sticky between us.

"It hurts me to have to say this," I told Verona, "but Kelly's always been her own person, and I long ago gave up trying to fight her. Maybe she's got a point too. She says it's got to stop—your presents." I didn't know whether or not the woman was even tuned in to what I was saying. "Are you listening to me?" I said.

She never moved.

"Well, you're going to hear me, because I'm the one who's got to say it." I was shaking myself, I'll have you know, maybe even a little bit angry because Verona just couldn't be civil. "Kelly says you've got to stop sending presents, because Mandy's getting old enough to wonder where they're coming from. That's what I'm supposed to say. And you know it's true. You've watched her grow."

42

Verona's eyes stayed down on the bread. She turned hard as the countertop.

"She's right, Verona. Mandy's no baby, but she doesn't have to know the whole story, not yet. You know that too. She's too young."

Miss Brigston from the second grade came through the door all smiles. "It's five minutes early, I know," she said. "But I figured you might not mind if I brought the kids down a little quick. They're so excited. Did you see the beautiful snow?"

I hadn't even looked outside since 7:00.

The week passed by, and Verona didn't say a word to me in all those days together. Everybody in this kitchen knew we weren't speaking—and they knew why too, even though I never told a soul, and neither did Verona. We're all grandmas here.

It's not easy living in silence. I went about the day-to-days and even laughed and joked with the others, but the whole Mandy business—and she's such a sweetheart herself—sat in my craw. It hovered over everything, every minute on the job, every last minute. But I wasn't about to break the silence, because it wasn't my problem. Maybe that was pigheaded of me too, I don't know.

On Saturday, Kelly was back at my house with a big box in her hand, fighting mad. "I took the jumper," she said, "but I'm not taking this—Christmas or no Christmas." She flung the box over to the couch, where it slipped off the pillows and fell to the floor. "It's got to stop. I told you to tell her, Mom. I told you."

When Kelly gets angry, her face sets hard as cement, almost like Verona's. She tries to mask her anger as if it's only determination.

"What is it?" I said.

"She must've paid a fortune for it. Look."

I put down my coffee, walked over to the couch, and picked the box off the floor. "Whyn't you stay awhile?" I said.

But she turned around and walked right out, leaving the door wide open. What was in the box was a magenta ski jacket with corduroy trim and a snap-off hood, Polartec, light as a feather—plus a matching hat and mitten set tucked into the hood. The price tags were all neatly cut.

Now they were both mad, I thought.

Kelly showed up at the door again with another box she set down on the step. "Take the whole

44

mess," she said. "I've had it. You talked to her, didn't you?"

"I mentioned it—"

"Then nothing's worked. She's pushed me too far now. I didn't want to do it this way. I tried to avoid it, Mom, you know I did. But she's driven us to it now—she has. It's her fault what happens."

"What's in there?" I said, pointing at the other box.

She gave the box a little kick. "Matching boots and bib pants. She doesn't even need it. We just got her the whole winter outfit ourselves in November."

I hadn't seen her so angry since she was thirteen, when I told her 11:00 was late enough, county fair or not. She'd spit then too. She's spit quite a bit in her years.

"Let me try once more," I said. "You just hold your horses awhile longer. You don't want to be Scrooge. Let me try again." Sometimes I think if Kelly would just cry, I'd feel less scared about her myself.

"All right," she said, "but once Christmas is past, it's got to stop." Mad as a wet hen.

"Don't you ever forget who she is," I told her. "Don't you ever forget."

"You're her grandma, Mom," she said. "I won't hear it."

"Then you won't hear the facts of life," I told her.

All she came for was to yell about the presents, that's all. "See you tomorrow at church," she said, and then she left again, just like that.

I tell you, I'd do anything for that girl, I swear, but she can grieve me no end—always could.

There I sat on the floor with my coffee up on the table, that cute little jacket all in a bundle, half out of the box. I picked it up and held it by the shoulders, then flipped the hood back. It was pretty, so little-girlish. I couldn't help thinking that Verona must have held it up before her eyes the same way. She must have pulled it out of the box it was shipped in just to hold it in her hands, to feel it, to let the whole sweet outfit inflate with Mandy's imagined body.

I got to my feet, kept hold of the jacket, and kicked the other box over to the coffee table beside the box Kelly had thrown. Then I sat on the edge of the couch and opened it up. I shoved my hand up into one of the boots, probably the same thing Verona had done, imagining Mandy's feet, warm inside against January cold.

The hat had stripes, with little tips like fingers. I put my hands into the mittens, and that's when I found the little brown bag. I opened it up, and a smaller bag fell out, a tiny plastic bag holding the thinnest gold necklace.

Oh my soul, Verona just couldn't stop herself, I thought. Even if she tried—even if her conscience told her that what I'd said was gospel truth—she just kept on buying because she couldn't stop. Giving those presents was all she could do for Mandy for eight years. I could just see her paging through JCPenney's—"this, and this, and this, and, oh yes, this too." She'd probably already had the whole outfit when I'd spoken to her a week ago. She probably took it all out that afternoon and laid it on the dining room table, the whole outfit—jacket over pants, hat tucked into the hood, mittens snuggled up into the cuffs on either hand, boots down at the bottom. And then she probably laid that gold necklace beneath the collar. She probably had it all in her closet since October already, two weeks after the winter catalogue first showed up in her mailbox. I know Verona.

It was my turn to host the girls for our Christmas party this year. It's one of those things you enjoy only when it's going on, not when it's ahead of you. Years ago, it would have kept me awake nights. I would have wondered what to serve and how to be sure everybody had a good time. But I don't care so much anymore; and now that I don't, I wish I hadn't got myself thick with nerves for so many years.

I made some chocolate pretzels and some blintzes and spread frosting over a host of Christmas cookies. I made a batch of sea foam and even a couple dozen gumdrops, and the whole time, I tell you, I ate way too much, way too much. I'll bet I spent twenty dollars on Chex mix, since my own kids eat it by the pound whenever they come over during Christmas—because I'm the only one who makes it with real mixed nuts. I took out the pinecone wreath from the closet and an old Christmas tablecloth that Ted claimed he didn't even remember. The only thing new for the party was a pair of Christmas CDs Ted picked out, only because he couldn't resist buying himself a new toy this year, that new CD player, when the tape deck he bought not that long ago still played very well as far as I was concerned. Boys will be boys.

It was Martha's idea to sing. Usually the girls each bring a five-dollar present, and we throw them in a pile in the middle of the room, pick a number, and everyone gets to choose—or trade. After that it's cards. But Martha says that this year we ought to sing a little for a change, since everybody likes to sing anyway.

"Whyn't you get Mandy over to play for us?" she said. "Didn't you say she was already playing carols?"

Now, listen. Martha plays ragtime like Al Jolson, by ear too. If she wanted to sing so badly, she could have played every last carol herself. There was something up her sleeve.

But I played the game. I asked Mandy to come over around 7:30 or so—it was a school night, after all—and play those carols she'd been practicing so all the cooks could sing along. By then, I figured, I'd have my sandwiches served, and we'd have gone through the whole presents thing. We all had a good time that night, even though Verona never said a word to me. I didn't try to pry her loose, because I think she's got a right to what she feels. We all joked with each other, we all had a good time, but the two of us never said a word.

And bless Kelly's soul. I can get so angry at that girl sometimes, but then she comes through and does something just like an angel. When Mandy came in that night, she was wearing Verona's black jumper, the whole outfit, even the yellow belt. She took off her jacket, and every one of the girls was just stunned. But Mandy is a beautiful child. I know I'm not to be trusted, being her grandmother, but I've got twelve and that makes me somewhat objective.

My Kelly's hair is dark and straight and cut short like that famous ice skater's. What hair Reg has left is thin and red. But Jeff has his mother's hair, blond as beach sand and very thick—and so does Mandy. She wore it up that night, in a single braid.

And we sang. We could have done a whole lot better with Martha at the piano, but grandmas don't really care much about their kids' fumbling. Mandy brought along her own book, a starter, so the melodies of the old favorites—"Silent Night," "O Little Town of Bethlehem," "O Come, All Ye Faithful," the only ones she knew—came out slowly in one-finger jabs.

And all of us, even Mandy, sat around the table afterwards, eating candy like none of us should. Twenty minutes, maybe, we'd sat there, when Martha said she had to leave.

"We haven't even played cards yet," I told her, but Martha got up from the table and went to the closet herself for her coat.

"I got big things to do," she said, "and tomorrow's Christmas dinner, the biggest meal of the year at school. But you just stay on here and have a good time, okay? Don't mind me."

See, they had it all arranged, the girls did. One by one they left—Anne had a brother over from Texas, Millie was worried about getting a call from her son in the service. They had it all arranged so that the three of us were left, Verona and Mandy and me. That was the plan, and I'd finally figured it out.

"I suppose I ought to be going myself," Verona said once Millie was up and at the door.

"You stay awhile," I told her. "It's still early."

Those were the first words I'd spoken to her in a whole week.

"Mandy," I said, "I bet Verona would like to hear those carols again. Whyn't you go over and play them—you two together. I got to do a little cleaning up here or Grandpa will have a fit."

I winked at my friend Verona, and she didn't have to say a word, because what was in her was written over her face in spades like it always is. She looked like a child again, with a face full of Christmas wonder. But it was all Martha's idea. I just played along.

I took my time cleaning up because what I saw on the piano bench—the way Verona touched that beautiful child for the very first time in her life, then hugged her when she made a little mistake somewhere—was just about the best gift I could ever have imagined. I love Mandy, maybe more than some of the other kids, the older ones sometimes for sure, but I got this great big joy in me from giving my darling granddaughter to Verona that night. It was Christmas joy, giving being the blessing it is. And that's something a human being never stops learning either, I'll tell you.

I let the two of them go for a long time, picked up all the food, did some of the dishes, even dumped the garbage, then I got out the present. I'd wrapped it up, complete with a bow, and I told Mandy I was giving it to her for playing for us, for all the cooks—for being our accompanist.

But it wasn't her eyes that I watched when her fingers fumbled with the paper. When Verona saw the necklace she'd bought herself, I put my hand on her shoulder to shush her up—and because I wanted her to look at me right then, at that very moment, to see my own eyes, so that once she saw my tears she'd know she didn't have to cry.

52

"It's beautiful, Grandma," Mandy said. "I love it. It's gorgeous." She lifted it out of the little box with her fingers and let it dangle. "I want to wear it," she said, and she turned to Verona without even thinking. "Can you help me put it on?"

That moment was Verona's whole Christmas, let me tell you. Nothing else, no present, could possibly come close. I can't tell you what I felt.

I shooed Mandy out the door at 8:30, already a half hour too late, but her mother never once minded time in her whole life, so she's not one to complain.

That left Verona and me.

She didn't say a thing. Her lips were shaking, and her eyes were glazed. She hunched her shoulders as if there really were nothing at all to say, and then she walked to the vestibule and pulled out her coat.

"Thanks for coming," I said.

Then she reached over and kissed me, hugged me too. I wonder how long it had been since she'd done that to anyone.

She had her hand on the knob when I remembered the jacket and the boots and the whole winter outfit. I could have let it go too, in the charm of that party and the blaze of joy in Verona's eyes. But I know there's more to life than Christmas candy, and I figured if my Kelly could dress Mandy up for her ghost grandma that night, then Verona could learn to bend a bit herself.

"I got some stuff here that belongs to you," I said. "I think you'd better take it along." I had the clothes in a couple of shopping bags on the floor of the vestibule.

She had no idea what it was. I know she didn't. She was still in a dream. She looked at me strangely, then reached down to slip open a box. I don't think I can really describe exactly what happened right then to my friend's face. Maybe the best way to say it would be that her heart got moved from heaven back to earth—but not to hell. She took this deep breath, as if the whole time on that piano bench she hadn't even taken a second for air. And then she bit her bottom lip and smiled. I know very well it wasn't easy for her to say anything.

"It's something how easy it is to return items nowadays," she said. "It's so simple, don't you think?"

"Wasn't always that way," I told her.

"Sure wasn't," she said. She looked up at me almost as if she didn't want to leave, but she did.

It was Christmas dinner at school tomorrow, after all.

Once she was out the door, I pulled out what was left of the chocolate-coated pretzels and ate all of them, every last one. Not once did I feel guilty either. It's no holiday at all if you've got to watch yourself every last minute. What's a holiday for, I figure, if not joy.

3 . . . The Gifts

She'll Love It

Smiling radiantly, the woman pointed at a table full of craft treasures: tiny Santas aboard tiny black matchbox sleighs on runners of candy cane, pinecones painted like snowmen, and twenty or so assorted Christmas tree decorations, each of them pretty and precious.

"The great thing is that none of them cost more than a dollar or two to make," she said. Even her frilly apron was cross-stitched. "God Bless You This Holiday Season" it said across her chest, the kind of print, deftly sewn, one might see beneath the picture of a horse-drawn sleigh in a winter wonderland. "A lot of these things are nothing more than trash, really." She picked up the Santa. "This guy is an old sock I would've used to wash my windows."

She laughed at her own joke. "My husband's old sock."

Julia sat on a folding chair with twenty other wives of school administrators, while their husbands—in freshly washed socks, she assumed—were busy in another room, talking about budgets. She'd never given two hoots about crafts, hadn't the time or the inclination to sit for hours with needle and thread. She was a captive to her husband's job tonight. Most of the administrators were men. Tom had wanted her to come along to the banquet, so she did, knowing full well that coming along probably meant sitting through something like this, some perfect housewife in frills explaining what could be done with baggies, old socks, worn panty hose, and empty Kleenex boxes—how to make treasures out of trash, for Christmas this time, the holiday meeting.

The lady had introduced herself as Melody or Melanie or something like that. "They make such wonderful gifts because you're giving something of yourself," she said.

Julia knew she was right about that. There likely was something special about giving some little thing you'd spent hours working on. But she never had that kind of time, not with her own teaching, her twenty-four second graders, kids whose noses ran daily during December, whose snow boots wouldn't snug up over their sneakers, whose zippers got stuck in their underwear; not with her own children, even though Amy was off to college and only Missy was around anymore. Pregnant Missy.

She'd bought Missy her first pair of maternity jeans on Tuesday, but that pair of pants had lain upstairs on the chest of drawers in Julia's own room because she couldn't bring herself to give them to Missy—Missy not even sixteen years old. So that pair of pregnant-lady jeans lay there beside her and Tom's wedding picture for four days, the crumpled edge of the shopping bag still bunched where she'd carried it in her fist for an hour in the mall; it lay there until tonight, not two hours before, when Julia knew she had to give it to her daughter.

"I could've had an abortion, you know," Missy said. "I could've just gone through with it and you would have never known."

That was probably true. She may well have lined up something on her own and taken care of the whole business like so many young girls did, even those as young as Missy.

61

"I'm glad you didn't," she had told her daughter. "It would've been wrong. You know that."

Missy sat on the bed with the nylon panel in her fingers, not crying—oh no, not crying, because their second daughter was too tough to cry—just angry, angry like she always was, angry at the world.

Missy had never told them she was pregnant. Somehow Julia just knew. It seemed strange to her that she could know as surely as she did, be gripped by the conviction that her little girl was going to have a baby. It was strange because Julia had never had a child herself. But there was this pudginess in Missy, not just physical pudginess either, but her hands were looking strange, her voice had lowered almost, as if she were a boy at puberty. And she was nervous, brittle in the way she could barely be spoken to. Not like Missy at all. Tough little Missy.

Julia had caught her at the door, just after breakfast, her school bag already up over her shoulder. Tom was in the dining room with his coffee. "Missy," she'd said, "I think you're pregnant. Am I right?"

Missy hadn't said anything. Just left for school. Walked out the door and never once turned around. Didn't deny it. So all that day, through second grade spelling bees and recess bruises, Julia thought about her daughter, a sophomore, having a baby—a baby she herself had wanted like nothing else in the world for all twenty-five years of marriage. In those early years of their marriage she and Tom had avoided department store toys at Christmas, kept themselves from the pain of seeing tractors and dolls and Tinkertoys, a pain so great that she couldn't speak of it. Tom had always insisted that there were thousands of couples who couldn't have kids, that it wasn't the end of the world; but she had given long stretches of her life, hours and hours, to unanswered questions about why it was that this woman's body of hers couldn't bring forth life.

The questions never stopped. Even when they adopted Amy, then Missy, and even when they brought those two little bundles home and laid them so carefully into cribs, even then the desire never left her, because she'd heard so many stories about adoptive parents who suddenly, out of nowhere, had conceived once the nervousness had passed, once someone else's child slept soundly beside them, just a wall away.

Now Missy, her own daughter, was fifteen and pregnant with a baby that she'd never once thought of conceiving—

"Everyone loves wreaths," the frilly woman interrupted Julia's thoughts. "If you walk in the woods at the lake you can still find pinecones lying all over. And they're so easy to make. All it takes is time."

Time was running out. Missy's middle was growing daily. That's why she needed the maternity Levis. But no one knew yet, no one but she and Tom. Tomorrow Amy would be home for Christmas. They hadn't told her yet because Julia told Tom it just wasn't something she could sit down and write. It wasn't some bit of news like "It's been terribly cold back home" or "The basketball team won five games in a row."

"Why don't you call her, then?" Tom prodded.

The thought of that kind of news out on some slender copper wire stretched from Wisconsin to New York seemed too public.

"No," Julia deliberated. "I'll wait. Amy will be home in a couple of weeks. Missy won't be showing yet anyway. She doesn't have to know."

"How can you not tell her?" Tom had said.

She and Tom were different that way. Tom was the one who had to talk, as if talking would make the whole thing go away. Years ago, when she couldn't get pregnant, he had told her to get some counseling—well, not told her, asked her in a loving way.

But the thought was the same: if you talk about it, maybe you'll feel better. But talking never made her feel any better about anything. Tom was like a truck full of cargo—once he'd gotten all of it off his chest, he could sleep. Just like making love. He was always the first to sleep.

"Just let me wait," she said. "I'll tell Amy when I pick her up from the airport."

"I don't know how you can sit on it that long," he said, as if it were some kind of explosive charge.

Maybe he was right. Maybe Tom was right about so much. She never knew. You get to feeling as if your mind is like a child's board game, a square-by-square path that angles and twists and winds around like a labyrinth because you're always second guessing yourself. Maybe what happened to Missy hurt so bad because she could never have a baby herself. Maybe it was simply selfish of her. Maybe if she had had children herself, she wouldn't be so constantly reining in her tears. Maybe it was her fault somehow. And in all of it she was forgetting Missy and her problems.

That's when she'd pray. Sometimes there weren't even any words, just grief and guilt and anguish that came out in a single question: why? And then a stream of self-doubts and wonderings . . .

65

Was it because she loved Amy more than Missy? She had always tried so hard not to be partial. Sometimes she'd be angry with herself for favoring Missy—overcompensating for what she knew but hated horribly to admit: there was something about Amy that was easy to love, something about Missy that was so very hard.

Was it her own frantic need for a child of her own when God himself had given her two healthy children? Maybe she'd spent too much time frozen in desire. Maybe she hadn't loved them, not really. Maybe she'd adopted two kids only because she thought they might be just what she needed to have her own. Maybe down deep she'd hated them, really hated both of them, because they hadn't delivered what she thought they promised.

And then: *why*? That one-word prayer, again and again. She'd waited for an answer from God. In the middle of the lunch hour, all alone in her room, her class outside in the snow, she'd sit, eyes open and staring, waiting as if somewhere on the blackboard God himself would write an answer. When the bell would ring, all twenty-four kids would bounce back in, their hands parched and red, stung by the cold. "Reading time," they'd say as they took their seats.

After lunch it was reading time, and for twenty minutes, surrounded by all those loving kids, she could lose herself in boxcar children and velveteen rabbits.

Maybe she wanted to teach in order to try to find that child she'd never had. She'd thought of that too. She'd thought of every angle—

"There are lots of places where you can get things laminated," the frilly lady interrupted again. "Look at these." She held up three placemats adorned with stick figures throwing snowballs and sledding. "I had my kids draw these. Then I took them down to the frame shop and had them laminated. I think they make wonderful Christmas placemats—even for Christmas dinner. And think of what Grandma will say—"

Just a few hours ago, Missy had been sitting there on the bed, holding the jeans. "I want to keep the baby," she said.

Julia and Tom had talked about keeping the baby before, but not for more than a half hour, because Tom had said it was not a good idea at all. She knew he was right. At fifteen, even with their help, Missy would lose so much of life that way. She'd graduate from high school with a kid in the terrible twos.

Julia and Tom could raise the child, of course, but it wasn't right.

"I don't think that's a good idea," she'd told Missy.

Missy laid the Levis on the bag and stretched her hands behind her. "It's my baby," she said.

"I know that."

"I mean, I don't have to listen to you because it's not really yours, is it?"

Julia pushed the Levis aside and sat next to her on the bed. "You're mine," she said.

"But I'm the one who's going to have the baby."

She took Missy's hand. "Honey, listen. Your father and I have talked it over, and we agree that keeping the baby just isn't the right thing." She squeezed Missy's fingers hard, bounced her hand on her thigh. "You've got to trust us."

"It's my baby."

"It's not a toy, Missy."

"But it's mine."

"It's God's."

"Well, that's easy to say. What's God going to do when it's dirty?" She pulled her hand away, lay back on the bed, then rolled over on her stomach.

Julia reached over and felt the soft denim. "God's got ways of changing diapers—"

"Don't be weird, Mom," Missy said.

"I'm serious."

She could feel the thump in the bed when Missy hit the mattress with her fist. "I want to keep it," she said.

"You're fifteen."

"So what?"

"You can't be a mother and be fifteen years old."

"There's lots of girls who do."

Julia felt herself about to cry, and it was always that way with Missy. Ever since she'd been old enough to think for herself they'd had disagreements, and every time they'd try to talk them out, it would be Julia who would be the first to break.

"You've got to trust me," she said. "You've got to trust your father and me."

"You're not even my real parents," Missy said.

At that moment it had taken Julia every last ounce of her strength to twist her body around and lie down next to Missy, to try to hang on to her daughter even when Missy was working harder than she knew herself to fling her own mother away. "I'm the only one in this room right now who loves you," she said. "You've got to trust me."

"I can't just give this baby away," she said.

"I know that."

They were lying there together, their two bodies across the bed.

"You don't know what it's like to have a baby," Missy said.

Julia had tried to be as tough and strong as her own little girl. She pulled herself up again and sat beside her daughter. "I know what it's like to have a child," she said.

"But you don't know. You're just getting back at me. You don't want it because you couldn't have one."

There they were at the bottom line, she and her dark-haired baby girl. She felt as if there were something tearing her out of that room then, something that wanted to protect her own daughter against what her mother might say. But she knew what was right. She held herself. "Missy," she said. "I don't care what you say. I love you."

Missy sat there with her face in her hands, her arms propped up beneath her. She wouldn't cry. She couldn't. If Missy would ever cry, it would be alone.

"That's all I can tell you," Julia said.

Missy stared at the eighth grade graduation picture tacked to the wall beside the bed. The silence felt like thick clay between them, thick, cold clay. But Julia had said everything she could say. She knew that. Now it was up to Missy. So Julia let the silence sit there like some half-formed wall between them, just sat and waited. She would have waited for hours.

Missy's hands dropped, stretched outward toward the wall, and she turned her face away toward the lamp at the head of the bed. Her bare feet swayed up behind her so her skirt fell in a puddle of plaid over the quilt. She was barely old enough to shave her legs, and somewhere inside her this baby was growing.

"Mom," she said finally. She swallowed something back. "Mom, sometimes I just want to die."

"I know, Missy," she said. "I know very, very well."

The woman in the frilly apron stood directly in front of the table full of Christmas treasures, one hand tucked beneath the elbow of the one that was gesturing. "As I've said before," she trilled, "these holiday decorations can be put together for hardly a cent. I'd guess

71

the whole table cost me no more than twenty dollars. And they make such great gifts . . ."

Julia had no time to make things.

When they drove home that night, Tom asked how it had gone.

"A woman showed us how to make decorations for Christmas," Julia said.

"Wow!" he said, guessing she'd be bleeding frustration. "Did you pick up any goodies?"

When she told him she simply hadn't heard much of what the lady had to say, he lost his gaming sense.

Julia said she wanted to pick up Amy alone, so Tom stayed home with Missy. He was refinishing an old oak commode in the basement, something he figured he'd give to Amy for Christmas. He wasn't so much in love with antiques himself, but on Saturday afternoons he enjoyed stripping down old pieces and making the grain redefine itself, all the time watching some ball game on the little black-and-white Julia had bought for thirty dollars and stuck downstairs in his shop. He called this therapy, but Tom was, in fact, far craftier than she was.

Julia didn't teach in Tom's district, not only because it would have been against the rules but also because she knew it wouldn't be a good situation. She taught in a town named Garland, about fifteen miles of old snaking highway away from Bartlesville, where they lived. In the five years she'd been back at teaching, she must have driven those miles a thousand times, so often that she knew the people she'd meet every morning at half past seven, even though she hadn't the slightest idea who they were or where they were going.

What's more, she knew every mile's worth of farms, from the abandoned home just outside of town, to the ramshackle place a mile from school where an old man tethered a goat to a front yard pole. There were old acreages and new A-frames on the steep, wooded hills that couldn't be farmed. Halfway between home and school, a tiny little place named Ranslik, a town of no more than two hundred, was slowly dying on the very spot where it had been settled a hundred years before. Nothing much more than a foundry there, just off the highway, its metal walls cast in a glow of orange from the rust that crept farther up every year, like red ivy, toward the cupola.

73

The old foundry stood on the banks of the Pecatonica River, a lazy old muddy thing that emptied into the Mississippi just less than a hundred miles west. By the Christmas season, the river was covered over with a foot of ice, and from where she daily crossed the bridge she could see the belted paths of snowmobiles that wound through naked lowland farm acres.

In a patch of woods on the hill above the river, an old leafless cottonwood jutted up above the trees around it, its silver branches reaching, like talons, into the sky. Every day Julia saw that tree, and sometimes she wondered why it hadn't fallen. Lightning had cleaned it of its bark, so it stood there like some skeleton, some symbol.

The tree had always looked to her like aspiration itself, like a picture of desire. The trees beneath it were content to be no more than what they were created to be, but this cottonwood had wanted something more. It had reached higher. But when it did, it was subject to the wind and rain and ravaging lightning. She saw herself in that tree—a woman rendered lifeless by her own excessive passion for a child, by her inability to accept the fate that the Lord had given her.

On her way to the airport, she passed the tree and wondered once again if it wasn't her own sinful jealousy eating away down inside of her, somewhere deeper than her hurt at what Missy had done, deeper than anger, deeper even than the fear of losing her. And again, right there on the road, she prayed for herself, for Missy, for Amy, for Tom, for all of them—her eyes wide open, her mind so tangled in emotions that she couldn't put anything into sentences; she prayed, knowing full well that God would hear the words in her sighing. And then she looked along the road, hoping for some kind of finger-painted message in the wide swath of snow clinging to the naked hills.

The airport was full of holiday traffic, carols ringing through the terminal like so much holiday clatter. She'd arrived just on time, but the flight had been delayed in Detroit, so she had an hour to sit.

She knew people who hated airports, but she hadn't flown often enough to dislike them the way others did, the people who carried or wheeled baggage around as if the place was just as familiar as a backyard alley. She walked through the gift shop, looked at the last-minute trinkets people bought. Sweatshirts, calendars, souvenir pens, fancy chocolate bars, a hundred different overpriced toys to satisfy any parent guilt-ridden for not thinking of his or her kids. She picked up a

Danish chocolate bar—two dollars for less than ten ounces—then took two and decided that she and Amy would eat them together on the long ride home.

The Lord had given them one perfectly lovable daughter. Amy was everything any parent would want—bright, mature, blessed with a loving disposition, talented, respectful. Amy and Missy were three years apart, but Missy had stayed behind a year in grade school. Amy had always tried to be a mother to Missy, another mother, and now that Amy was coming home, Julia was afraid of how she would react to what had happened. Amy was likely to walk into Missy's room and tell her where she'd gone wrong, not in a righteous fashion either, just honestly and lovingly. But it would be something that Missy didn't need from her always perfect older sister.

She looked up at the monitors once again, at the flashing time behind Amy's flight number, then checked her watch and walked over to the gate where the plane would arrive. It was always a shock for her to be in the airport. There were so many people, all of them nameless, all of them moving back and forth constantly, people always leaving and always arriving. Hundreds and hundreds of people, so many of them absorbed in magazines or some airport novel, or just walking, walking, walking. She sat across from a man wearing a bolo tie and a cowboy hat. He wore one of those half-pairs of glasses, and he was reading *Business Week*.

People began to gather around the gate adjacent to Amy's, groups of people in families ready to welcome some member back home. Julia could read anticipation on their faces. She wondered how she looked to the others, whether it was clear on her face that all of this reception wasn't only Christmas joy.

A whole battery of young couples maybe thirty years old were standing and sitting around the east edge, some of the men staring out of the window and holding their kids as if trying to be the first to spot the plane. They were friends. *You can tell the way friends talk with each other because it's not forced,* she thought, *it's not just so much small talk, so much being polite.* In Tom's job there weren't always such good opportunities for friends. His job was lonely. She had friends herself, of course, at school, but she didn't live in the district, so "they" as a couple didn't have friends, not friends like the couples who were there at the gate together.

Four couples. All of them well-to-do. You could see it. The men looked clean and well-dressed, the women proud of themselves without being pompous. Two of the women were holding hands with a woman standing between them. Two old couples were there too, like grandpas and grandmas, all of them waiting together, it seemed.

Julia thought there was something nice about airports, something nice about the hugs and kisses at the gates. She'd hug Amy too when Amy came in. It was always so easy to hug Amy. Even when she was a child, she loved to snuggle up—next to Julia or Tom—with a little book. She loved to be held on a lap.

At a nearby gate, a whole group of people was waiting, all right, everyone waiting for someone. Some of them had children. Some of the kids were tugging away at their fathers' pant legs, pointing at the gift shop or water fountain or some other attraction. But they were all together, like a large family. *Maybe there's a European tour or something just getting over,* Julia thought. *Or maybe they're all from the same church.*

She leaned back in her chair and thought about eating her chocolate bar. She reached in her purse, then decided to wait for Amy. The man in the half-glasses had fallen asleep across from her, the magazine folded against his chest.

From out of nowhere she heard the announcement for an incoming flight. It registered in her mind because she heard the voice say—it was a woman's voice—"Gate twenty-two," which was the one right next to Amy's.

The couples rose simultaneously. The women still held hands. It was odd, Julia thought, the way they held hands like that, as if it were grief they were holding back. The woman in the middle looked back at her chair to be sure that a package she had taken was still there. It was precious.

Julia decided to get up and walk over there. It wasn't more than fifty feet. She would watch the package for her. The woman in the middle wanted someone to watch the package for her. It was something Julia could see in her eyes.

A uniformed man opened the door to the gate. The first people off the plane were businesspeople. Julia could tell it by the way they folded their London Fog coats over their arms, by the way they toted their bags, and by the fact that no one was there to greet them. Then came the others: college guys in Levis and sport coats over madras shirts, college girls with fancy earrings, holding the kinds of books you can't buy in airports.

Julia looked down at the package beneath the seat to make sure it was there.

The woman stood over at the door, waiting. All the couples stood around together. One of the grandmas hugged the woman. Her husband came over and took her hand. When she looked back at the package, Julia waved her fingers just to let her know that she was watching her things. The woman smiled nervously, almost as if she were crying, but happily.

Almost every passenger had deplaned when what the group was waiting for came in a perfectly white bundle of receiving blankets—a baby, a brown-faced Korean baby, all wrapped up as if it had just come from a bath.

It was a child they were waiting for. All of that love, all of that anticipation, the nervousness, even the thin tears around the woman's eyes, all of it for this child. The woman carrying the baby handed it to its new mother, as if the bundle of blankets was the most precious gift in the world, then slid her arms out carefully once the mother held the child firmly in her arms. Then she kissed the mother, and the grandpa kissed the mother, and the husband kissed his wife, and everybody kissed and hugged, and Julia stood there keeping watch over the package at her feet.

Tears flowed more easily now. The husband dabbed at his wife's eyes with his handkerchief because she couldn't reach them herself, and she didn't seem to care anyway because there was no reason not to cry. She simply stood and held that child, stared into its round, brown face as if by noting every single wrinkle and line she would bring it into her soul. And Julia knew exactly what was in that woman's mind, because she saw herself there once again, holding both of her children, both Amy and Missy, for the very first time, in pure disbelief that this child—that these children—could really be her own, their own, Tom's and hers.

The woman suddenly looked up as if she had forgotten something very important. She stared at Julia, at her feet. And Julia picked up the bag and brought it to her.

The woman held her bottom lip in her teeth and smiled, her tears washing down her cheeks. "Thank you," she said when Julia brought her the package. "Thank you. This is my baby."

"I know," Julia said. "I know."

"Will you get it out for me?" she said.

So Julia reached in the bag and took out a tiny stuffed bunny. "He'll love it," she said.

"It's a girl," the woman said. "She's a girl."

Julia didn't want to be crying. "She'll love it, then," she said, remembering how she'd waited in the schoolroom and she'd waited on the road, watching blackboards and stretching fields of snow for someone's clear handwriting. But now she knew that God had given her the message here in the airport; and it had come in the tears she felt brimming in her eyes, the tears of a mother who never was and yet was, even today; the tears of a grandmother who would give her own child's baby away into arms no less loving than these that hugged all around. To see it, to remember, to know again, was God's own gift to her at Christmas.

An hour later Amy came bounding off her flight, third person off, before the businessmen, a huge student bag flopping around her shoulders. Her hair was cut short—short and kind of sassy, a little too short maybe—her face bright with anticipation.

"Mom," she said, and the two of them hugged the way people do when it means something to hug.

"Oh, Amy," Julia said. "It's so good to have you back."

Amy pulled herself away quickly, poked her lower lip out with all the resolution in the world, and held her mother at arm's length. "It's so good to be home. I know it's going to be a good Christmas, Mom," she said. "I just know it."

"So do I, honey, so do I," Julia said, because she could feel grace in her arms, her fingers, and in her heart; grace that strengthened her, built her up once again the way only the Lord can do, grace in a brown-faced gift of love.

4 . . . The Church

Finding Something

"We've not *found* anything, Mom."

That's what Ellen had told her, and how many times hadn't Ellen said exactly that when she had asked the question? "We've not found anything, Mom"—a reply at which Jan might have felt hopeful if the words weren't twisted in the same way every time Ellen said them. "We've not *found* anything, Mom." Emphasis on *found*, as if to say "end of discussion." That answer always came packaged in a deadbeat tone that carried too much finality, and Jan knew (aren't mothers supposed to know?) that Ellen wasn't really looking at all.

So she'd tried once again, Christmas Eve. "Have you found a suitable church?"

The two of them were about to go to bed. She'd come for the holidays. She'd not looked forward to a long plane ride to Seattle alone, now that Jack was gone. She'd not looked forward to the trip itself, but she'd crossed the days off the calendar because she wanted so badly to see her kids, her smart kids who were making so much money in computers—Microsoft this, Microsoft that. She'd never been to their new place, a flashy condo with windows for walls. But she couldn't help asking again, as if the topic had never come up before—"Have you found a suitable church?"

"We've not found anything, Mom," her daughter said in a computer voice. And then Ellen gave her a smile that Jan knew was condescending because, after all, she was "Grandma" and the two of them, her son-in-law and daughter, were big shots—corporate jet, power lunch, lots of travel. Ellen and Frank were cutting edge, and Jan was an old oak buffet from Iowa.

She wanted to tell her daughter that the two of them weren't going to find a church if they sat on their hams or slept in to catch up from work weeks that had them gone more than home, their kids hostage to some preschool with a big cheery sign with multi-colored balloons.

"Have you been looking, Ellen?" she'd asked her daughter.

They were wrapping presents. It was Christmas Eve, mind you, and they were still wrapping the kids' Christmas presents. Frank was in his office—they each had one in the big condo—and the kids were off to bed.

"We've looked," she said, fitting a corner on a whole box of electronic games. "We keep telling ourselves we've got to slow down," Ellen told her. "We've got to smell the roses, you know? Last summer we were out on the boat only once."

"Whose fault is that?" Jan said.

"Ours, of course," Ellen told her.

"Are you still in love?" Jan said.

"Mom!" Ellen scolded.

"I'm serious," she'd said, curling the ribbons across the top of Tosha's new Barbie.

"Look, Mom, we're all right, okay? I've never stopped thinking that there's a God. I'm no infidel."

After that first insipid smile Ellen never once looked up, which Jan read as a good sign, like there was some guilt there anyway. "Maybe we ought to go tomorrow," Jan said.

Ellen dropped her shoulders.

"I'm just suggesting—"

"I'm thirty-four years old, Mom," Ellen interrupted.

"I brought you into this world," she said. "I know exactly how old you are." She flitted with the ribbons, put the gift under the tree, and sat back on her haunches. "I'm serious. I saw this church—"

"You just got here."

"I saw this church on the way in—not big either. 'Ten forty-five' it said, 'Christmas Service.'" She looked directly at her rich daughter. "You and me and the kids? Frank is your responsibility, not mine."

Ellen rolled her eyes, threw her bangs back out of her face. She looked down at her fingers, pushed back her cuticles, breathed audibly. "Let me think about it, okay?" she said grudgingly. "If that's the way you have to have it, let me think about it."

And now Jan couldn't sleep. She lay in a roll-out bed in her daughter's office, the light from some fancy screen saver bouncing off the walls because Ellen didn't have the grace to shut the stupid computer off. *That machine is more important than I am,* Jan told herself when she tried to keep out the glimmers. But she knew Jack would have been proud of her. In all those years of their daughter's unfaithfulness to God and the church, Jan had been the one who constantly begged him to give Ellen space. But Jack was gone now. Just her bringing it up—going to church—was something he'd have been proud of.

The screen kept shifting images like something that wouldn't die. She hated it, the lit screen that devoured everything good and right in the lives of her own children. The room was dark, the blinds pulled, and that fiend machine kept turning multicolored 3-D shapes inside out in some never-ending pattern that seemed to her demonic. The clock said almost 3:00 when finally she got up, hunted for the plug, and then jerked it. Didn't hesitate a minute. Just jerked it. Tomorrow she'd plead ignorance, since that was what they thought of her anyway. Jack would have loved it.

The death of the computer didn't help. Ellen would be more upset, she told herself. Pushing church on her was one thing, but killing computers was a whole new level of sin. Jan would be lucky if they didn't stick her back on the jet. At least it was dark in the room, she thought. At least the walls didn't jump. Fanciest condo she'd ever seen in her life too. All sorts of pottery things in shapes she didn't begin to understand.

It was August when she and Jack had prayed, as they did every night at supper—"bless Ellen and Frank and the kids" and usually something else about helping them find the way because, after all, they just hadn't *found* anything, had they? It was August, and hot, and Jack had insisted on digging up the concrete around the pole he'd put in so their son Tony could shoot baskets when he was a boy, years ago. It was too hot, and it was too much work, but Jack loved sweat, considered himself more of a man if he could soak a T-shirt. They'd prayed for Ellen and Frank after supper, then he'd gone at it again out back, where she saw him an hour later, on his side, not moving. Their last prayer together, like so many before, had been about Frank and Ellen, had featured them, in fact. It was as if they'd never stopped praying.

"Lord," she said now, her neck strained from such a huge pillow beneath her head, "Lord, help me find something for them." That seemed about right. "Lord," she said, but she didn't know how to put it better. "Lord," she said once again, "crack their skulls, okay? I don't mean it really, but stop them in their tracks. Sink the boat, maybe sink Microsoft, okay? Because there's nothing here, I'm afraid. There's just nothing here. Something's got to break. I love them too much, and I love my grandchildren." In the middle of that prayer, she imagined those kids in a darling Christmas Eve pageant, two sweet kids saying things like "Mary pondered all these things in her heart," Tosha with a little skirt, Edmund in a sweater over a white shirt or something. There were churches all over Seattle, hundreds of them just waiting for families like Ellen's. Thousands of churches.

"You can lead a horse to water, Lord, but show them you're here, okay? Make it so that everywhere they look they see Jesus." She hadn't even thought of saying that, but when the words ran back through her mind, she liked it, the idea of seeing Jesus in everything, as if the world were a canvas holding the outline of Jesus's face, as if the whole world were the Shroud of Turin. "Make them see you, Lord," she said, "because in this palace of theirs, well . . . I just don't know if you're here."

She didn't end the prayer. The petitions just sort of fell into silence, like they always did, to be picked up again next time, same chapter and verse. Pray without ceasing, the Bible said. That's what it was, all right, she thought.

93

When she awoke, she heard the kids stirring at the tree, opening presents, arguing, in fact. She brushed back her hair, pulled on her housecoat and slippers, and opened the door. It wasn't quite fully morning, but the kids had all the wrappings off of dozens of presents. Too many. It wasn't pleasant.

She walked into the spacious living room, the blinds over all those windows to the east still closed.

"What's the deal?" she said.

Tosha said Edmund had taken her Beanie Baby and hid it somewhere and she was mad and she was going to get back at him somehow because it just wasn't fair and he was a jerk too and always was. It was Christmas morning, and Edmund was looking at his sister as if she were a dishrag.

Jan had enough. "Maybe we ought to go to church," she told them, out of nowhere at all. "You and me—maybe the three of us should go to church together this morning."

"Why?" Tosha said.

"Because it's Christmas," she told her. "Because it's Christmas, and we're going to celebrate the birth of our Savior."

"I'm not going," Edmund said. "I got these great toys."

"You've got a great Savior," she told her grandson.

His eyes, blank as clay, hurt her more than a fist because she knew she was speaking a language he didn't understand. Their own grandson looked at her as if Jesus were a nobody. That Jack couldn't see this was a blessing.

Edmund shoved his glasses up on his nose. "Maybe some other time, okay, Grandma?" he said. "Look at this—Nimbus Racer." He held up an electronic game.

She wanted to pray, right there in front of them, but right then, even though the condo was top floor, she was sure there was nothing but thick cement between her and the Lord. The children didn't know a thing. They hadn't *found* anything, all right. They hadn't even looked.

"I think we ought to go," she said.

"It's Christmas," Edmund chirped. "Why do we got to go to church?"

Her insides felt like that screen saver, turning inside and out again and again, and she realized just then that if she were to open her mouth, there would be no words, only tears—tears that would confuse

95

them. So she walked to the kitchen, fiddled with the coffee maker, got it going, then went to the west windows.

It was Christmas morning, she reminded herself, and she couldn't help but wish just then that she were with Jack and the Lord. There was too much for her to do here, too much hard work and too much sadness, and she couldn't do it alone.

She took hold of the strings of the blinds and opened them with a few rapid jerks. Sunlight, Christmas morning sunlight, spilled in like a waterfall, dousing the lights on the tree. Deliberately, she looked away from Christmas in the condo and over the street beneath them, then past the trees, then across the glaze of water west. And when she raised her eyes to the mountains, in a flash, in a moment, the whole fancy condo seemed to disappear: the Christmas tree behind her, the kitchen, the brewing coffee, everything behind her seemed to vanish, the children's voices dimmed, her own sharp fears muted in the sheer majesty of what she'd suddenly, almost magically, become witness to. Because even though the neighborhood beneath the condo was in shadows, the sun coming up far behind them stretched its brilliant glory through the crystal morning air all the way across the Sound to hold those monstrous snowcapped Olympics in its own astonishing splendor. There they stood—those glorifying mountains—as if forever. There they stood like might and power. There they stood, a landscape divinely painted across the darkened world, beaming holiness and majesty in the crystalline dawn of a perfect Christmas morning.

"Oh, my God," she said, because what she saw was far more than mountain beauty. He was here, all right, she told herself. He was here sure enough.

"What, Grandma?" Tosha said, coming up behind her. "What do you see?"

She wrapped her arm around her granddaughter.

"Who's out there?" Tosha said on tiptoes.

What could she say? "Jesus," her grandma told her. "He's always there."

"Where?" Tosha asked.

She picked up her granddaughter. "Look at those mountains," she said. "Just look at them."

Tosha leaned her face closer to the window. "Is he a ghost?" she said.

"No," she told her. "He's alive."

"I don't see him," she said. "I see the mountains and I see the Sound, and there's a boat out there, but where is Jesus?" She looked at her grandmother almost painfully. "Grandma, I want to see Jesus."

She already had her granddaughter in her arms, so the hug she gave her wasn't difficult or awkward. "Amen," she said, biting her lip, because a prayer she'd never finished was coming to a close maybe, even if just for a moment.

"Let's just you and me go, Tosha, honey," Jan said. "This time, this morning, let's just you and me go. I want you to see him too."

5 . . . The Pageant

First Cry in a Stable

That I wholeheartedly agree with Kathy Simpson about oversentimentalizing Christmas does not change the fact that Ms. Simpson is not my favorite human being. She gets her way by sheer force of character. She's great to have on your team. Oppose her, and you lose.

"There's an awful lot of silliness connected to Christmas celebrations already, and we don't want to add to them," she said. She held forth at the end of Christmas pageant practice, and she had all the kids—shepherds, wise men, Mary and Joseph, the whole works—in the first two pews for her address. "Animals singing and all of that? It only sentimentalizes the real story: that Jesus came for us, for sinners." She barely paused for breath. "Did he cry? Well, of course he did. He was human. Humans cry. Case closed. So this foolish little line, 'No crying he made,' is just ridiculous, sentimental hooey."

I knew how my daughter would take that remark. For most of her thirteen years, Angela has considered *The Lion King* the greatest story ever told.

"Jesus was born in a barn because, quite literally, there was no room in town." Kathy pointed in the air. "Have any of you ever *not* found a motel? It's awful. Jesse and I were in Athens, Ohio, once, years ago, and we couldn't find a thing, but that's another story."

Thank goodness, I thought.

"And Christmas carols in the mall? That's probably the biggest sacrilege of all—'The Hallelujah Chorus' as Muzak."

My daughter has no idea what Muzak is.

"That's why we have to be authentic—as authentic as possible—because we don't want to sentimentalize Christmas."

Angela understands the word *sentimentality* no more clearly than she does the unpardonable sin. I'm sure she rather likes hearing "O Holy Night" in Wal-Mart.

"And that's why we have to make the truth stick—"

I thought Kathy Simpson's choice of words somewhat inappropriate because I knew what was coming.

"Angela," she said, pointing right at my daughter, "you live on a farm."

Angela would never want to be thought of as a "farm girl."

"We've got to have some manure."

Angela would rather incinerate her *101 Dalmatians* video than touch manure.

"Shepherds were tough hombres," Kathy told the kids. "Shepherds were lowlifes, and God sent his angels to them for a reason: because they were lowlifes—that's the point of Christmas. He came to save ordinary people—not just kings but the lowlifes."

Kathy wanted just a bit of manure in church. Her request had been a big deal five years ago, raised a big stink, in fact. But Kathy Simpson wins her battles.

"We need manure on the manger. We need it on you guys, the shepherds. We need it around the church— or something that looks like it," she said, like the field general she is. "On Christmas Eve this isn't going to be a church, it's going to be a barn."

Angela, the manure pipeline. I knew she didn't like the appointment in the least. That's why she was growly when the lecture ended and she got in the car with me.

Besides, my Angela wanted to be Mary, but Roberta Dekker got the job. On a scale of ten, Roberta Dekker is, I'm sad to admit, a nine to my Ang's six. Ang didn't want to be a manure-caked, cross-gendered shepherd, especially if Roberta got Mary's song. So all the way home, my daughter didn't say a word; not until I pulled into the garage did her mouth open at all, and then it became my fault. "Who's idea was it anyway for us to move to the sticks?" she said.

My daughter still has the sentimentality of a child, but time and her own body chemistry are pushing her most unmercifully toward adulthood, and complexity, a place where she really doesn't want to go.

We bought her a horse this Christmas, but we gave it to her already just after Thanksgiving. I thought there was a verse in the Bible that says your young women will love horses. Angela is on speaking terms with Macintosh (she named it after a computer?), but all this schmaltzy *Black Beauty* stuff? No way. At least that's what she puts on. Actually, I think she likes him, even if, in front of her parents, she acts otherwise.

I've been in the barn with the chickens several times and heard her talking to him. It's our having moved out of town that irritates her. She thinks she's miles from her friends.

Angela hovers on the precipice of being an adult, and, like the coyote in Road Runner cartoons, a fall is inevitable. I remember the first time I took her to the dentist, and Dr. Lowell, a kindhearted guy, stood there in front of her and told her she was going to have to watch the sweets—take it easy on candy. She couldn't have worn a heavier face, but back then the poor kid had no sense of darkness. Today, she does. And it's the mix that confuses her, like it does all of us. She could get along swimmingly in a child's world of light; I think she could, like all of us, learn to negotiate her way through the darkness, if darkness were forever the shape of things. But it's the mixture that's tough, and that's what she's learning. She still would prefer her Christmases much more, say . . . Norman Rockwell.

We opened our presents during the afternoon of Christmas Eve this year. Randy, our oldest, home from college, brought Lexie, his girl—but, as Kathy would say, that's another story. At Christmas, my wife, whom I love dearly, loses control. She claims there's ten times as many great presents for a boy like Barry, our youngest, who's ten, than a girl like Ang. Besides, Barry's her baby. So this year, when Angie's major-league present was a horse far too big to corral in the family room, when her little brother looked over a range of Christmas booty that threatened to take over the house, and when her big brother Randy and his sweetheart fiddled with his new DVD player, Angela looked down at some tatted hankies from Grandma, a study Bible from her parents, and a new sweater, and felt indecently shortchanged. She left the house in unthrilled silence.

Now, a word in defense of my daughter. It really wasn't a lack of presents that got to her. She knew very well that Macintosh was hers and hers alone. What bummed her out was a lack of climax. A day after Halloween, the march toward Christmas begins. Everywhere you hear music. Christmas specials air nightly after Thanksgiving. Angela, the child, lived in anticipation of something called "Christmas." In her mind, that "Christmas" reaches its climax around the tree when we open presents. That Christmas Eve afternoon, the ritual of presents simply didn't deliver the goods, didn't live up to the hoopla. She wasn't as much angry with us as she was let down by a drum roll that had risen to this very day and then simply whimpered away.

We moved to an acreage for many reasons, but one of them is critters. I love animals. Kathy Simpson wasn't wrong—we've got manure in all shapes and sizes. So getting some was my excuse to go out and talk to my daughter. If the nativity scene was going to grip us with authenticity, I'd have to collect the dung. Ang wouldn't. No way.

I suppose I shouldn't have been surprised that she wasn't with the horse when I got out there. Instead, I found her with the chickens, sitting cross-legged on the floor in her sweatshirt and jeans.

My daughter is becoming a woman. Her shoulders have broadened, and even with her in that seated position I could begin to discern an hourglass.

We had been losing chickens, five of them in five days—a couple of leghorns, a Rhode Island Red, and then the one that had really angered me—a Buff Orpington, a fluffy and fat brown honey of a hen, if chickens can be likeable. The identity of the murderer was a mystery—the victims were hardly touched, just a plump hump of feathers, necks split. Coons we've had before, but a raccoon doesn't simply drink blood.

I didn't have a clue what was doing the cold-blooded murders when I put out the trap.

Ang had been furious at the killings, but not because she likes chickens—sometimes I have to push her to get the eggs. She had told me that if whoever or whatever was doing the killing would eat the chickens, she could tolerate the murders. But such wanton killing galled her, and she wanted the murderer's blood. I was mad too. When I saw that Buff down, I would have taken on a skunk with a straw broom.

That Christmas Eve, as we were opening presents, the murderer had arrived and walked into my trap, and there he was in front of her.

"What is it?" she asked me when I came up behind her.

The animal was long, and blessed—graced—with glossy fur. It looked up at her nervously and paced back and forth, back and forth, like the king of beasts.

"Good night," I said, "it's a mink."

"Are they rare?" she asked.

"Not rare, but wily. I never thought I'd catch a mink in a box trap. This one must be retarded."

She pointed. "He doesn't look retarded," she said. "He's gorgeous."

And he was. His tiny eyes were translucent in a face that looked classic, Greek or Roman. Nimble and agile, his body flowed through that cage. Like a cat, he showed no expression, and the stoicism granted him an astounding nobility. He was brown . . . no, chestnut . . . no, reddish-mahogany, with a sheen of darkness over the ends of each follicle of warm, beautiful fur that even in the soft yellow light of the coop shone like the red planet. He was beautiful. "You can see why people want coats," I told her.

She was transfixed, as if that mink were an alien. "Can we keep him?" she asked.

"It's not a sheep, Ang," I told her. "You're lucky enough to see him. They're nocturnal. I don't know what brought him in so early—must have figured the place was a piece of cake."

"You think he did it?" she asked.

"I *know* he did," I told her, pointing at the dead leghorn across the room.

"Look at him. I can't believe he's a murderer," she said. "Why should he? He's too perfect, Dad. He's just beautiful."

"He sucked the blood out of five hens," I told her.

109

Back and forth, back and forth, the mink ranged through the trap.

And then she said what was really on her mind. "I've been thinking, Dad—you know the story—about what happened?" For the first time, she looked up at me.

"About 'what happened'?" I asked.

"In the stable in Bethlehem?" She shrugged her shoulders, annoyed at what she'd sounded like. "Seems as if you can't even say anything about Christmas without it sounding like a commercial."

"What happened?" I said.

"That old story—I know it's silly and it's dumb and it's not in the Bible. You know that old story about how all the animals in the barn suddenly spoke at Jesus's birth?"

"I know the story," I said.

And then she looked back at the murderer, the beautiful mink, and pointed. "You think it was all of them who spoke?" My daughter had wanted this thing dead, but when he appeared in his unforgettable coat, she'd fallen in love. "Even a mink?" she said. "You think they all spoke?"

"It's just a story," I said.

110

"But let's just say it happened," she said. "You think they all spoke or sang or whatever, all of them?"

"Every last one," I told her. "Every last critter in the neighborhood, even the killers."

She nodded knowingly, like someone who was no more a child. "It's a big deal, isn't it?" she said, and I don't think she meant that as a question.

"You mean Christmas?" I said.

She nodded again. "Christmas," she said, and then she brought her hands right up to the cage, half an inch away, held them there as if she could hold that beautiful mink herself. "You know what the Bible says, 'The lion lies down with the lamb,' isn't that right? Something like that? Isn't that the way it goes?"

"You got it," I said. "At Christmas everybody sings." And then, very patiently, I asked her, "So tell me this, Ang: you get it, don't you?"

Her back was to me. I couldn't expect much more than that. She didn't turn to face me or look at a church full of people or anything. She was staring at the killer and thinking of the most beautiful nativity music, thinking of peace, of a silent night full of cartoon voices. Nobody else saw what she did just then, but I did, and I won't ever forget that one definite, glorious nod of her head.

111

And here's the miracle I observed on the night of the great miracle: a stunningly beautiful killer mink on Christmas Eve prompted my daughter's first public profession of faith.

"Let's go back inside," I said. "They're all waiting. It's Christmas."

"No kidding," she said, like a child, but I swear that what I heard from my daughter just then was the voice of a woman, a woman who will, I'm sure, soon enough be given a much bigger role in a much greater pageant.

She didn't hold my hand, but the two of us walked together from the barn to the house. Midwinter, the broad prairie sky sparkling with the jewelry of stars, and I swear, something very much like a chorus of angels somewhere up above.

6 · · · The Afterglow

Merry Madness

If she had remembered what Wurzburgs looked like two days after Christmas, she wouldn't have brought the kids, she told herself—hundreds of people with too much money, pawing merchandise and forming return lines dozens of customers long, all sorts of grousing. A madhouse. A scramble of people, none of them happy, even though Christmas was still in the air. On December 26th, she thought, the monster humanity comes stalking back out of hibernation. The lights are put away somewhere, and there's no more "Silent Night."

A popcorn popper and two sets of new plastic tumblers, all of it extra and piled in Wurzburgs bags, were stacked in her arms, which made the going even tougher. What Bethany Home didn't need could be returned for good money. Lord knows they needed good money. This time of year, any money at all, for that matter, she told herself.

At least the children she took along would stay with her. She'd had that much foresight, anyway—take only those kids who wouldn't wander. She hoisted the packages up in her arms once more and turned completely around. Tony shadowed her, like he always did. Sarah and Clarisse were holding hands, Clarisse poking her tongue through the brand new gap between her front teeth.

"It doesn't hurt, Aunt Mary," Clarisse said.

"That's wonderful," she said. "Just like I promised, right?"

They were moving up the escalator toward the fourth floor, where the returns desk was located. Beneath them, the men's department was swarming with women rifling through sweaters and shirts. Little Laney stared out over the scene beneath them, quiet as the little mouse she always was, both her hands in her new Christmas muff.

"Too many people," Aunt Mary told her. "Too many people for my taste."

Laney pulled a hand out and pushed the fur back from her matching hat in order to see Aunt Mary. "Did you see my daddy?" she said.

What she'd learned was that kids could say anything, anytime. Who knew what "Did you see my daddy?" really meant? Laney could have meant anything. "I didn't see him," she said. "Did you?"

"I saw him," Laney said immediately. "My daddy works here. He paints signs. Did you see him?"

Mary's immediate reaction was to leave, even though they hadn't returned the gifts. Get out. Laney, their little emotionless beauty, didn't need to see her father. Even though Mary didn't know him, she'd been in the business long enough to guess what the guy was capable of, long enough to know that if he was working right here—right here in Wurzburgs—and he didn't want his daughter, he couldn't be much of anything.

"You're sure?" she asked Laney, and the little girl nodded her head again.

She had no idea what Laney's father looked like, no idea where he lived. She pulled the packages up in her arms, glanced to the top of the escalator, then looked back at Laney. The little girl's face registered no shock, no surprise, no fear, nothing but the same grayness that had been there since the afternoon she'd arrived at Bethany weeks ago.

"I have new teeth," Sarah told her, showing off.

"Pretty new teeth," Mary said quickly. She reached down, the popcorn popper under her arm, and brushed Laney's cheek with the back of her glove. "Honey," she said, "did you really just see your father?"

Laney pointed back over all of the third floor.

"He works here?"

More nodding.

Mary turned to watch her step as the escalator brought them up to the fourth floor. "Be careful now," she said to all of them. "Don't slip. Hold Aunt Mary's coat." She nodded toward Laney. "Just hold on, sweetheart."

She walked the girls away from the returns desk and toward the furniture department, where she found a huge sofa, sat Sarah and Clarisse down, then her packages, and knelt beside Laney. "Honey, I want you to tell me the truth. Did you really see your daddy?"

She nodded. "He saw me too," she said. "He went like this." She curled the ends of her fingers in a surreptitious wave.

Mary had never considered the possibility that one of them would spot someone from their family—never. The city was too big. And you couldn't worry constantly either. The kids would never get out if every last time you took them somewhere you had to worry about who they might run into. Still, she thought, Laney didn't need this—didn't need to run into him. Mary took Laney's arms in hers, hugged her. "Did he wave at you, honey?" she prodded. "Did he say anything?"

Laney pulled her right hand out of the muff and pointed. "He draws them signs," she said, pointing at a sale placard on a green rocker.

"How do you know it was your daddy?" Mary said. When Laney hunched her shoulders, she knew it was a stupid question to ask. "You're sure?" she asked again.

Laney nodded again, still looking away.

It was her grandparents who'd brought her to the Home, who had said only that the little girl needed to be out of the fray. Her grandfather kept shaking his head, even though he had done most of the talking, his wife standing behind him with a balled-up handkerchief, repeating over and over how good it was of Bethany to take their little dear. "This is just temporary, you know," the grandpa had said in the adult voice grandparents often use to say things that allow kids to continue to hope.

"I bet your hands are warm, aren't they, Laney?" Mary said, taking a hold of the muff.

Laney nodded.

"Did you have a good Christmas, honey?" Mary said. She looked for anything in Laney's eyes—fear, anticipation, joy, regret—any emotion that would indicate her feelings about her father. "And your little hat is so pretty," she said, but there was nothing on Laney's face, only the flat, claylike stare she'd seen so often, something that she'd come to recognize in some kids, something that lay like a lid atop emotions often unseen. There were times she wished Bethany Home had taken only older kids so the kids could explain what they felt. Little ones like Laney didn't even know themselves.

"Maybe when we go back you can introduce me," Mary told her.

Laney's cold gray eyes swept away from the crowd of people emerging from the escalator and for the first time focused intently on Aunt Mary's face. Once again, however, she simply nodded.

"You'd like that?" Aunt Mary said. "Would you like to talk to your daddy, honey?"

Laney loosened the strings of her new Christmas hat. She seemed to have no fear, but it would be better for everyone, Mary thought, if they went back to the car via the furniture and out the back of the store. She'd already spent too many nights nursing fears that seemed to arise out of hope that so often crashed. Laney wasn't making things up. That wouldn't be like her.

Already, maybe, she'd made far too big of a deal out of possibilities. Already, they'd stopped because Laney had thought she'd seen her father; already the afternoon had piled up because of what might have been. At all costs she wanted to avoid what her questions alone could have already created. They had to keep going. "We'll never get out of here if we don't get rid of these things," she told the kids, starting the trek over again and leading the girls toward the returns department.

The clerk looked over the boxes, unopened, then picked up the popper, turned it in her hands, and asked for receipts.

"They're gifts, all of them," Mary told her. "We're an orphanage, and these are extras—doubles, you might say."

121

The clerk's rather significant nose gave her a mean look, but after checking through the opened boxes, she pursed her lips, nodded, and said, "No problem."

Returns weren't the problem anyway, anymore. The specter of a father was. If Mary decided to deliberately avoid the possibility of Laney seeing him again, what would that say to Laney? That Aunt Mary didn't care about her father? Well, she'd have to chance that, because there was simply too much to risk in letting Laney see her father again, of raising hopes that were sure to be dashed. Really, Mary had no choice.

The clerk with the sizeable nose scribbled notes down on a pad she'd drawn from the drawer.

On the other hand, Mary thought, maybe it would be best for Laney to see him—unnatural for her not to. There was no injunction, no court orders. The grandparents had dropped her off. "Just to be out of the fray," they'd said. Maybe she wasn't the occasion for warfare. Maybe she loved her father. Mary glanced back down at Laney. Nothing seemed clearly registered on her face—no dread, but no anticipation either. Stoic, as always.

Playing God was something neither she nor Marguerite had imagined doing when they started the Home. In their visions, the work seemed simple enough: create a place for homeless kids, a place for the two of them to give the love of Jesus to children who rarely felt anything. Every night they'd have dinners around tables full of food; every night they'd read books to the kids, and every night the children, unwanted children, would fall asleep in their care.

Several months before, they'd talked about it one night when the kids were asleep, about what it meant to be responsible for the well-being of the children, about how they'd never quite estimated how much that responsibility would cost them, inside. Back then they had only five or six kids, but they'd already found themselves making all kinds of horrendous decisions about children's lives.

"I don't think I can do this forever," Mary had said. "The job is too big."

Marguerite fished what she could get from the grannies at the bottom of the popcorn bowl in her lap. "At night it's so good, though, isn't it, when all of them are asleep?" she said. "Every night I thank God for giving us what he has here."

"And every day?" Mary said.

Marguerite looked at her and grinned. "And every day at least once I ask myself why we got into it in the first place."

They both laughed.

Marguerite offered her what remnants remained in the bowl. "We both know why, Mary. They've got no one else. These children are ours from the Lord. They've got no one on their side but us. That's why."

The returns clerk smiled. "God bless you," she said, "and the children." She handed back the refunds, then reached down beneath the counter and produced four candy suckers, hiding them carefully. "May I?" she asked Mary.

When Mary said it was okay, she handed one to each of the kids, red and green for Christmas, but Mary insisted they each put them in their pockets for later, but she knew Tony couldn't leave it alone.

Her arms emptied now, she took Laney's hand in one of hers and Clarisse's in the other, trusting Sarah to be the little mother she already was, then headed for the back of the fourth floor, Tony just a step behind. She'd thought she'd avoid the big rush by staying away for at least a day after Christmas, but there were hundreds of people, all of them lugging boxes and bags, most of them far less than joyful now the holiday was past. She aimed for the elevator back behind home furnishings, thinking it was just plain sensible to avoid some kind of scene. The kids in tow, she steered through the shoppers, not hurriedly but determinedly. She'd nearly lost her breath when she came to the elevators, but when she looked back Sarah and Tony were gone.

She stooped down quickly. "Did you see them?" she said, and just as quickly she stopped herself from saying any more. If she shouted, Laney and Clarisse would get upset; if she didn't, Sarah and Tony would bawl for sure. She kept hold of the girls' hands, swinging in and out of rows of plates and glasses.

"You're looking for these two, I bet," a man said, and it took her less than a second to realize that the man was Laney's father. Maybe it was the stillness in his face, the lack of fire.

"I'm her dad," he said, pointing, and then quickly dropped to his knees beside his daughter. "What a beautiful muff, honey," he said.

Laney nodded, smiled politely. She didn't throw her arms around him. Plainly, she was pleased but not overwhelmed.

"Did you get it for Christmas?" he asked.

She nodded again, greeting the attention with the same cold stare she'd shown when she first announced she'd spotted him.

Even though she and Marguerite hadn't been in the business long, Aunt Mary had all she could do to fight hatred welling up in her, hate she knew wasn't at all Christlike, hate for this father-who-was-not-a-father, hate for what he might have done to his daughter—for what he did do, giving her up, letting her go like refuse, something he didn't have time for. She hated him for missing his daughter's Christmas. She hated him for anything he'd done that day because he wasn't with his daughter, hadn't called, hadn't written a card, hadn't visited, hadn't brought as much as a candy bar. And there he sat, petting the furry muff as if it were a kitten.

"It's beautiful," he said. "I bet it keeps your little hands warm, doesn't it?"

He was dark, like Laney, thin and small, hair falling shadowlike over a small forehead, tiny hands, almost delicate and not at all rough, his voice gentle

126

as a girl's. His thick eyebrows arched over deep, piercing eyes—and he looked for all the world like a fine man, she thought, like a real father. That was the horror—that neglect and abuse could come from someone who looked this good. It was something she'd seen before, something she thought she'd become used to.

She'd already come to understand that hating him—hating them—was a luxury she couldn't afford, because no matter how many nights she would tuck Laney into bed, no matter how often she would read the child a story or wipe tears or a runny nose, she knew she would never play his role, never be Laney's miserable failure of a father or mother. That was something she had to respect, even when mothers and fathers, for whatever troubled reason, didn't.

"She looks nice," the man told her, looking up. "She looks cared for," he said. "You're taking great care of her." He reached for his daughter's face with his fingers. "Daddy's going to come and see you," he told her. "Tomorrow maybe—how'd that be?"

Aunt Mary had to fight the immediate impulse to scream. She wanted no more empty promises. What she would have loved to do was pull the little Bible out of her purse and make him slap down a hand and swear, right then and there, that he wasn't giving Laney some promise he didn't intend to keep. Too often that happened—too often. When she looked at him, she tried to tell him with her eyes, to press her hate into her stare. "Don't you tell this precious little jewel that you're coming if you don't intend to." That's what she would have loved to say.

"You're on Fountain Street, aren't you?" he asked her. "I've seen the place, I think, somewhere around Central High?"

She nodded, not wanting to say a word, not wanting to open her mouth even the tiniest bit for fear that what would come out would be something the children should never hear.

"Used to be a pub, right?" he said.

"Used to be a pub," Mary repeated.

He looked back at his daughter and snugged up her collar with both hands. "Listen, sweets," he said. "Daddy'll come out to see you, okay? Bring you a present. Didn't get you that present in time for Christmas, did I? I'll bring it yet, I swear."

Don't you swear, Mary thought. *Don't you swear or I will.*

"Fountain Street," he said again, almost like a question. "I've seen the place. I'll be there."

She didn't believe a word of it, even though this man clearly was no failure. Shaved and clean, his hair sharply cut, he seemed polite and even refined, she thought, someone who knew very well that his daughter should be at home, not at Bethany, especially this time of year, especially at Christmas. When she and Marguerite had decided to start the Home, what they'd considered was the love, not the hate. What they'd wanted were the orphans, not the parents.

Slowly, the man pulled himself to his knees, then his feet, keeping his hand on his daughter's shoulder. "This run of bad luck," he said, "I don't know how long it's going to take, but her mother and I have to get some things straight." He reached down for Laney again, and Mary could feel his fingers herself, like thistles. "It hasn't been easy for me," he said. "I want you to know that—being away from my angel."

Laney never once smiled at him, not once.

When he kissed Laney's cheek, Mary held herself back for a moment and then said, "We'll be expecting you." Straightforward—straight on, not backing

129

down a bit, she said it. "Laney will figure on you—today yet?"

The man glanced up at the clock. "I got time this afternoon?" he asked himself. It was almost 4:00. "Maybe not today anymore, but tomorrow probably. If not, Thursday for sure. I'm not kidding."

And then something happened that surprised her. Laney swung herself away from her father's arm and leaned toward Mary, both arms extended. She would have fallen between them if Aunt Mary hadn't taken her in her arms.

"Terribly busy in the store this time of year, for me too. Tons of new signs, you know, after Christmas and all," Laney's father said. "Hey, listen," he said to Mary, "let me give you something here, okay?" He reached for his wallet and pulled out a dollar. "Here," he said. "Give it to the Home. You deserve it."

Aunt Mary could have cried.

Waking the children that New Year's Eve was Marguerite's idea. To Mary it seemed more than a little frivolous and not even healthy. But Marguerite insisted that her parents had always allowed her to stay up when the New Year came, and she remembered what fun it was. She said they shouldn't be too frumpy about things; after all, hadn't the state inspector said that if there was anything wrong with Bethany it was the fact that things were altogether too neat? Mary didn't really think it was possible to be too neat.

But she was not in a mood for big celebrations. Laney's father hadn't shown up on Thursday, although he'd said he probably wouldn't. But he hadn't shown on Friday either, nor on Saturday, nor even on Sunday, when some of the other kids went home for a visit. He hadn't shown up at all, so Aunt Mary had come to think of him as demonic. After all, how could anyone be so deliberately injurious, so deceitful, so pitiless to such a beautiful child. His own.

Nor was it Aunt Mary's idea to feed the children bakery goods at such a late hour. All that dough would sit in their tummies like sandbags, and later on they'd all be up with tummy aches. But the smell of the oven invaded the place; Marguerite wouldn't be put off, even though Mary reminded her that those warmed-up, day-old pastries were meant for the holiday.

"Tomorrow they'll be two days old," Marguerite had said, tying her apron. "Tomorrow I'll bake something fresh. Just go get them up, Mary," she said, pointing toward the children's rooms.

It was almost midnight, and it seemed like a sin to rouse them. What was the difference anyway between this midnight and any other on the calendar? she asked herself. Where in the Bible did it say for anyone to celebrate New Years?

She walked down the hallway and opened the door to the girls' room, then waited for a moment until her eyes adjusted to the darkness. They were all asleep. Marguerite had made such a big deal about the coming of the New Year that Mary had been sure none of the children would shut an eye. She stepped in, the door still open behind her and the light from the moon on the snow outside filling in the dark corners of the room.

Clarisse—a war baby, unwanted when Daddy returned from Korea.

Sarah—Mom had been killed; father had left long ago.

Nan—abandoned.

Marne—the most beautiful eyes.

Karen—already with them two years, like a big sister to the others, even though she was only twelve.

Laney—the quiet one, silent as stone.

Every night Mary had waited for Laney's father. Every night she'd anticipated his visit. She had told Marguerite about running into him in the store, about him actually hunting them down just a few minutes later, but she didn't say that he'd promised to come. That's how sure she was he wouldn't show. Besides, why tell Marguerite, who would likely tell her not to get her hopes up. So every night she watched Laney's face when she'd put her to bed, watched for a grimace, a tear, something to show what the child felt about empty promises. But Laney never asked about him. Nothing seemed to register in that child, nothing showed on the outside, over her face. Sometimes as Mary held the girl in her arms, she wondered whether in fact it wasn't herself who needed the man to show up, needed him to renew her faith, not in God, but in man, in humankind. The world had begun to seem so full of sadness.

Down the hall she heard music.

Marguerite had turned on the radio. Loud. Mary leaned over the bed Laney shared with Karen and rubbed Laney's forehead with her fingers. "Girls," she whispered loud enough for all of them hear.

Sarah shot out of bed as if she hadn't been asleep after all.

"Put on your housecoat," Mary said, but Sarah was already out of the door.

Karen rubbed at her eyes and insisted that she hadn't been sleeping. Clarisse asked some half-sleepy questions that made no sense, something about the tooth fairy as she pulled her housecoat from the hook on the back of the bed. Marne, last as always, sat up and whimpered.

"What's the matter, honey?" Mary said, holding Laney in her arms.

"I'm so hungry," Marne said.

"Aunt Marg's got something really good," she said. "Just go look."

Laney was a doll, cuddly and soft but lifeless, almost inert, wanting to be held but never hugging anyone, her eyes like a doll's always open and staring. There seemed no possibility of holding her enough, yet she never asked to be held, never asked for anything.

"The New Year is coming," she whispered to Laney, and the little girl nodded her head in approval. "Get your housecoat on and come on down with the rest of us. It's such fun," Mary said, releasing her. "The New Year is coming."

Marguerite had the most ridiculous thing on the radio, Mary thought as she woke the boys. New York City—all of it a party too, and the man on the radio was talking about how many minutes were left in the old year and how people in the streets were standing around and kissing each other and drinking liquor. And Marguerite had it on the radio so the kids could hear it too.

"Open the doors," Marguerite said. "Open the doors and windows, Mary!"

"It's dead of winter outside," Mary snapped.

"Just for a moment," Marguerite told her, offering her warm doughnuts. "Go on," she said. "Get the windows. On New Year's Eve the city rings bells and sirens, and some people blow firecrackers."

"Can we go outside?" Sarah said.

"You may not!" Aunt Mary said, and Sarah dropped her bottom lip halfway to the floor.

But Marguerite did not wait for Mary. She swept through the parlor and the living room and the play room, throwing open the doors and the windows as if life itself stood just outside. The man on the radio—

and my goodness! was the volume up high too—kept counting down: "Twenty-five, twenty-four, twenty-three, twenty-two, twenty-one . . ."

Sarah and Clarisse were hugging like two kids who hadn't seen each other for years. The boys were in a circle around a whole cookie sheet full of warm, day-old long johns and pastries. You should have seen Markie's cheeks—he looked like a squirrel. And Tommie Lee didn't need the extra weight either, Aunt Mary thought.

"Thirteen, twelve, eleven, ten . . ."

And then Laney came to her, as if afraid of all the activity. She came to her in the chair and snuggled in her lap, like a cat tucking her little feet beneath her.

"It's almost time," Aunt Mary said.

In her hand, Laney held a chewed hunk of glazed doughnut.

"You like sweets, don't you?" Aunt Mary said.

Laney nodded.

Out from some closet, Aunt Marguerite produced an old derby hat they sometimes used for costumes. She wore it jauntily on her head as she passed among the kids with another tray full of goodies.

"Eight, seven, six . . ."

And at that moment Laney turned toward her, her eyes lit brightly for what seemed the very first time. "Aunt Mary," she asked, "which door?" She bit her lip slightly. "When he comes, where will we see him?"

The pain Aunt Mary felt at that moment grew from a place so deep within her that she felt nothing could stanch its bleeding.

"Where, Aunt Mary?" Laney said again, full of excitement, chewing on the doughnut, her eyes on the front doors.

What could she possibly say? *Lord God in heaven,* she prayed, *what can I tell this poor, innocent child?*

As if to try to stretch the moment, as if thinking maybe if she waited another ten seconds the right words would come to her, Aunt Mary simply asked a question—to stall, to give herself time, with God's help, to find a way of talking to this beautiful child who never, until this moment, had smiled. "Who, Laney?" she said quickly. "Who's coming?"

And just like that, Laney said, "New Year," as if it were so very silly of Aunt Mary to ask. "New Year's coming, Aunt Mary, but in which door?"

And at that moment something emptied from Aunt Mary's soul, something heavy with dread and fear and even hate, something she'd recognized long

137

ago as evil, because it was something of despair. It squeezed out from her heart in boisterous laughs strong enough to cover what might otherwise have been tears falling all over that child's pink housecoat, tears of happiness.

The room was full of noise. Aunt Marguerite scrambled around like some cheerleader, holding the children's hands in a circle, all of them dancing in front of the Christmas tree. How on earth would they ever get to sleep, Mary thought. The radio blasting. Outside the bells and sirens of the city making all kinds of silly noises.

Right in the middle of that merry madness, Laney pulled herself away and, without looking back, jumped to the floor and flew off to the side of the room, where the windows and doors stood open to the winter, as if this was Florida and not Michigan. Without missing a step, Aunt Marguerite grabbed Laney's hand and pulled her in with the others, then winked quickly as a whole string of them played an impromptu New Year's version of London Bridges.

Marguerite signaled Mary to join in. Nothing could have made Aunt Mary happier. She got up from the rocker, kicked off her house slippers, and pointed to the doughnuts.

"In a minute," she said. "I'm starved."

Soon enough, the whole living room was freezing, full of love.

7 . . . The Snowfall

Joy and Miracle

I am not a Picasso, a brutal misogynist who inflicted terror on nearly every female around him. Neither am I a Hemingway, a drunken lout given to baring his chest and knuckles at the drop of a hat. I adore Van Gogh, but I would not cut off my ear for anyone. I respect the dramatic accomplishments of Elizabeth Taylor, a woman who's gone through nearly as many husbands as she has major roles. To my mind, Tolstoy is the world's greatest novelist, even though he was impossible to live with.

I am an artist, but I don't think of myself as a social misfit or a study in pathology. I believe that art requires balance and design, commitment and zeal, the diligence of our closest attention, but not insanity or bizarre antics. I do not take the stage unprepared. I believe I know Willy Loman, even though he never existed anywhere except on paper. I have done Hamlet's soliloquies with such fierce regard for the young prince that even today I could do "To be or not to be" and wring passion from my own hesitations.

I adore grand opera, Brahm's *Requiem*, and anything by Verdi. I wouldn't think of spending a Christmas without Handel. I once thought Andrew Wyeth too garishly ordinary, but he haunted me until I couldn't resist him, and now my home is filled with his paintings.

I despise kitsch and almost everything sold in media stores, save the Bible, most of C. S. Lewis, and a few CDs no one else buys. Most of rock music I find to be noise. It's difficult to believe that television could be even more of a wasteland than Newton Minnow called it more than three decades ago, but it is. Most of evangelical Christendom's antics, from California Magic Kingdoms to the nearest suburb's faddish mega-church, I find unseemly.

I'm sorry. I'm not nice. I don't like smiley faces or annoying people who say, "Have a nice day." Health concerns aside, I won't eat fast food. In my fifty years,

I have become conditioned to believe that whatever America thinks *cool* will soon be seen as silly.

I am, as most of you may have guessed already, unabashedly elitist.

I chose the church I attend (at first) because of its architecture. Its unobtrusiveness in the surrounding hilly wooded landscape seemed a tasteful reminder of the quiet importance of deep spirituality. I found the place a delight. The preaching is thoughtful, the earnestness understated. Most of all, I appreciate the fact that the people I've come to know there really do like each other. I've met several of them, and they're not showy or pretentious. When you enter Deer Valley Church, people don't hang on you as if church were a discount shoe market. You're not a mark at Deer Valley. I like that.

This year they asked me to narrate their Christmas program. They gave me the script, and I read it. I found it slightly zealous but acceptable, even unassuming. It was a retelling of the old story, and it demanded a big voice, they said. I have been in theater for most my life. I teach theater at the university.

I appreciated the manner by which they asked. They told me they knew I was busy—and I am. They told me they felt the whole evening would be a triumph if they had someone with my presence to read the part. One of them said, "We can get by without you, but we'd love to have you. It would be an honor."

I couldn't say no.

I was raised in a religious home, and as much as I love art and the theater, I've always felt that my serious religious upbringing was something to be honored. I've always thought of God as the only first-rate artist. There's so much that's miraculous about us—the way three tiny bones in our ears can process sound waves, for instance; and around us his perfect hand has painted the greatest masterpiece, the ecology of nature with its balance and precision, the way it can juxtapose competing forces into something harmonious. Stop and look sometime at the beauty of a weeping willow—I can go on and on . . .

I have never denied my need for God. I have, like many, forgotten him for considerable portions of my life, but he has not forgotten me. So I told the people from Deer Valley, the church I attend somewhat more than occasionally, that I would read the script for their Christmas program. I may have preferred T. S. Eliot, but the performance, I knew, would not be an embarrassment.

There is a kind of magic to theater that some will never know. Its attraction is not simply the applause. The lighting must be perfectly cued to pronounce every bodily gesture. The words, of course, must be masterful; content must be borne on sound that comes as close to music as anything unscored. One stands before an audience that is shrouded in darkness, awaiting the story; and when the drama is delivered, when it's done with the passion required to communicate the text truly, the result is something very much alive.

And that's what I felt that night when we offered the Christmas presentation. Perhaps it was my own mystery, this man who visited the church often but sought little other than worship when there. Perhaps it was the script, which was, when I started to read, more effective than I'd thought it would be. Perhaps, simply, it was Christmas—no other season of the year quite so conducive to joy and miracle. But we started almost blissfully in touch.

I stood on the proscenium and delivered my opening narration, the text before me, and the place was stone silent. The audience read every turn of my head, every flashing smile, every narrowed eye. When it's all perfect, what happens in theater is love, an act so

147

intimate and selfless that sometimes I see a guarded-ness arise in an audience, as if they fear that they're risking too much by falling so completely into the design of the dream I'm offering them. At that moment, they need to be surprised again into reality, deconstructed so as to assure themselves that they are still where they thought they were, and that I am worth their trust. It's a dance, a wonderful dance, and in the opening minutes of this Christmas drama at Deer Valley Church—for whatever reasons—what happened between us was quickened by love and devotion.

When I finished the opening, I walked to the back of the pulpit area and took a seat. Beside me, three adolescent girls from the choir were seated on the floor, while some younger children sang their hearts out in front. One of the girls had a string in her hand, a long, looping string that she gathered between her fingers in an intricate weave. The others watched and laughed, giggled and nudged each other, even though the children were singing.

I never married—perhaps that was a mistake. But I believe my devotion to my work would never allow me to give enough of myself away to another human being. So I never had children, and I don't think I understand them. I am convinced, after teaching for twenty years, that our entire society has gone mad in the homage it pays to them. We have created a whole generation of kids whose education in self-esteem has spoiled them rotten. I have few students willing to commit to the craft; the ones who are are often the children of immigrants or the poor.

This disruption right beside me—the girls obviously didn't care if I heard them—stayed with me like a plague. I grew up in an age when it was an honor and a privilege to have the stage; but to be up in front, part of the choir, meant nothing to these kids. They kept whispering and giggling, as if what we were doing that night wasn't at all important.

I pushed my foot over to the closest of them, kicked her behind just slightly, then gave her an ogre-like look when she turned toward me. She did not stick out her tongue, but the face she gave me made it very clear that I was out of order in expecting she might listen to my admonition. Her lip went down in a sneer that said, "Who do you think you are?"

For the rest of the night, through all of my recitations, I never achieved the union I'd had with the audience in that first scene; and the reason was simple. I knew there were three girls behind me who simply didn't care. My intonation became strained, my pacing was gone—the shepherds, the glorious assembly of angels, the story of the stable, the young mother's love, all of it came haltingly after my silent confrontation with the giggling girls. I knew they didn't care, and, in my mind, that killed the performance.

I don't know that I can completely explain my anger. Perhaps those who have never worked at art will not understand. Those three girls wrested my attention so completely away from what I was saying that, in the process, they became my sole audience. I delivered lines in a voice meant for them, even though they were behind me and probably never for a moment stopped chatting and playing with that loop of string. And the longer it went on—through the whole course of musical interludes, the recitation of the children, the five long narratives I offered—the more angry I became at their insolence. The more bitter I felt.

When it was over, I was relieved but seething. The lights came on following an a capella rendition of "Silent Night." But my irritation grew over me like a disease I felt in every pore, and when I left the front of the church I wanted only to get out.

A number of people—many of them—thanked me for what they considered a great performance. I nodded and smiled politely. And then an old woman came up, a woman I've come to know somewhat through my visits to Deer Valley, a retired missionary, a small and unassuming old lady with shaky hands and eyes bright as stars, a woman who must have read Luke 2 a hundred thousand times and spent her entire life telling it, over and over again to children in the Far East. She took my hand, pulled me down toward her face, and gave me what the Scriptures call a holy kiss.

"Your reading," she said, "it was wonderful." I cannot describe the grace of her smile. "It was as if I had never heard that story before," she said. "You made it new." And then she nodded and was gone.

That stopped me cold. *I had made the old nativity brand new to a retired missionary?*

I have performed on stages throughout America. I have done countless seasons of summer stock, dozens and dozens of performances in repertory. I've done Shakespeare and Tennessee Williams, directed O'Neill and Moliere and August Wilson, but in all the theater I've ever done, I never before had considered myself a vehicle, a messenger, a conduit. I'd always thought of what I was doing as what *I* was doing.

That night, though, with the touch of a holy kiss on my cheek, I had a new sense that I'd been used as if I were an hourly employee of the business of the gospel. Even in my weakness, I'd been a strength, if only to one old woman who I would have assumed to be less in need of the gospel of love than most everyone in that small church on Deer Valley Road.

When I left that night, what I discovered was that the God of nature had created a masterpiece. Lake-effect snow fell like a blessed assurance of Christmas. There's a quietness to new snow that bravely muffles every last sound of the city. The cones of light falling from street lamps seem netted in snow. The pines were festooned, dressed for celebration in white robes. Footfalls puffed on the sidewalk. Bethlehem may be desert country, but in the Midwest, Christmas is only Christmas when it's clothed in a mantle of purity.

I drove myself home, alone, this odd experience still shimmering in the night's white darkness. In my mind, I had failed. I hadn't been the master I pride myself on being. I was only a servant. I wasn't an artist; I was little more than material—imperfect at that, burdened with an ego bursting with petty grievance. I was used that night.

And that's when it hit me, this epiphany of Christmas. He came for those who need him, not because they are poor or slovenly or unable to care for themselves. He came for all those who need him, even some like me, the elitists, self-satisfied with the arrogance that insists they really need nothing at all. He came for me because I too—in my annoyance and pride—am very much among the needy.

A hundred times or more I've cried on stage. It is a technique that, with practice, one accomplishes quite easily. But alone, in my car, the holy kiss still there on my cheek, I found myself suddenly in company with the Lord who came to earth, not for Christmas, not just for spoiled children, but for all of us, even me. He made me a blessing, even in my pride. He washed the sin of my human arrogance in his blood and through me made the story new, both to an old woman and a proud old actor.

At that moment I felt something totally unpracticed pinch my eyes and choke my breath. I wasn't acting. The Lord of heaven and earth was acting upon me.

Come, Lord Jesus.

A professor of English at Dordt College, **James Calvin Schaap** lives in Sioux City, Iowa, with his wife, three children (one in-law), and two small grandchildren, who make the season bright.

He's the author of more than twenty-five books, including the critically acclaimed novels *Touches the Sky*, *Romey's Place*, *The Secrets of Barneveld Calvary*, and *In the Silence There Are Ghosts*. His work in literature continues to receive awards and attention, including two Iowa Arts Council fiction honors.

His articles, essays, and short stories have appeared in more than twenty-five leading magazines, journals, and anthologies such as *Poet & Critic* and *Mid-American Review*.

His most memorable Christmas occurred when he was ten years old, he says, when his parents hid his first full-sized bicycle, a white-walled J. C. Higgens, behind the couch, then threw winter coats over the back to cover the protruding handlebars. That's where he found it on Christmas Eve, a moment of startling joy he's never forgotten.

That old bike is long gone, but his own startling joy, he claims, is even more full of wonder with each passing year.